# LIVING
## AGAIN IN
## GOD'S
## ABUNDANCE

# LIVING AGAIN IN GOD'S ABUNDANCE

*Strength & Comfort
When Your Journey Takes
an Unexpected Turn*

## SUZANNE DALE EZELL

A
JANET
THOMA
BOOK

THOMAS NELSON PUBLISHERS®
Nashville

*A Division of Thomas Nelson, Inc.*
*www.ThomasNelson.com*

Published in Nashville, Tennessee, by Thomas Nelson, Inc.

### Library of Congress Cataloging-in-Publication Data

Ezell, Suzanne.
    Living again in God's abundance : strength and comfort when your journey takes an unexpected turn / Suzanne Dale Ezell.
        p. cm.
    Includes bibliographical references.
    ISBN 07852-6511-2
    1. Christian women—Prayer-books and devotions—English.
2. Consolation.  I. Title.
    BV4844.E99 2002
    242'.643—dc21                                    2002000870

*Printed in the United States of America*

02 03 04 05 06  BVG  5 4 3 2 1

To my two handsome sons,
Chase and Jason,
who are my strength,
and also my weakness

# CONTENTS

# ACKNOWLEDGMENTS

$\mathcal{D}$ave Shepherd continues to head my list of acknowledgments. He helps suggest, create, and polish the product, and then takes it to market. Without Dave there would not have been a first book, or a second book. Thank you, Dave.

Appreciation to Janet Thoma who in her wise way directs the project, keeping it on the path to success. And much appreciation to Jenny Baumgartner, my Nashville editor who helps with details that pull the final project together.

My love, my gratitude, and my admiration go to my mother, Mary Dale, for her strength and her steadfastness throughout all my trials and tribulations. She is a strong, self-assured, wise woman of age who rarely gets her due.

For special help in this project, I wish to acknowledge my friend and daughter, Sara, who inspires me every day as I see her handling challenge after challenge to create a bright, sparkling, and charmed life. She is also my computer guru, heavily supplementing my woefully lacking technical skills.

Much love and many thanks to Bud and Regina Dale—my family of origin, who have such a special way of encouraging me and always "being there" for me. Their Texas ranch is an oasis for tired, spent writers.

Lives are lived in community. And this book was written in community with many fantastic women. Accolades and sincere thanks to the legion of women who contributed their stories and ideas to this collection. They have consistently reinforced the theme that you can overcome obstacles to build a better life. I'm sorry I couldn't give you their real names and more personal data. I wanted to protect their privacy and the privacy of their loved ones. But I truthfully can tell you that if you knew them, you would love them as I do.

And to you, dear reader, let me say, *welcome!* Welcome to my world with all the tears and pain, as well as the ecstatic happys! I met so many of you personally and through letters from the previous book. So I feel we are all mostly old friends, sitting down for a chat. I appreciated the call I got one day from a reader who said, "You don't know me, but I just finished reading the chapter in your book about June 11 being your sister's birthday. I know it makes you sad she is no longer with you. I just realized that today is June 11, and I wanted to call and tell you I was thinking about you!"

See what I mean? *Welcome!*

*The winter of the soul had come, too soon, and without warning.* —MARGARET JENSEN

My absolute favorite moment of the year is the Christmas Eve service at church. There is a point in the service when all the lights are turned off and we begin to sing "Silent Night, Holy Night." Then in the total darkness of the moment, the speaker lights one candle. The tiny flame of that one candle is so bright and so beautiful, it takes my breath away.

The *darkness* enhances that light to expand its illuminating power far beyond the size of a single, small flame.

Then one by one by one, we each light our own candles, and the church begins to glow in candlelight. But without the darkness, the brilliance of that first candle is diminished. Which is to say, when I truly experience the goodness of God, I must experience Him through the wonders of darkness as well as in the light.

At the end of my previous book, I was sitting smugly on the top of a grassy knoll, enjoying the warmth of the sunshine as I looked back on interesting experiences from my life. The assortment of highs and lows—each had its own system of survival. I was contentedly looking forward to enjoying the autumn of my life, "the harvest," I said, "the fruits of my labor."

My three wonderful children were grown and in the process of making their own homes, so I felt that my work was largely done. I could sit back and simply enjoy watching each one continue to grow and flourish.

Our daughter, who had been born with a crippling bone disease, had graduated from Vanderbilt, and had even added a graduate degree. She was well on her way to a career with the university. Both of our sons were educated, had launched their own careers, and were enjoying abundant lives with only limited input from Mom and Dad.

Life was good! Yes, I enjoyed sitting on that imaginary grassy knoll and being thankful for all that had gone before and hopeful for all that was yet to come.

But in the midst of this peaceful pastoral scene, the storm clouds were looming on the horizon and rapidly gathering momentum. As the last word of that previous book was penned, the first clap of thunder sounded.

In short order, the loud, dark storm expanded to full force. *My thirty-five-year marriage was ending!*

Instead of savoring my life from the top of a warm and grassy knoll, I found myself standing in the darkness with my whole world crashing down around me. Every image of myself, every role I played— every value, every hope and dream—crashed like a huge and very violent storm.

For weeks, it seemed that as each twenty-four-hour period passed, another giant tidal wave came down full force across my shoulders. Or was it a super-speed train wreck hitting me? I really couldn't tell. My only memories of those days were incredible pain and immobilizing darkness.

Thirty-five years gone. Also gone was my beautiful home, the special tulip bulbs I had planted last fall, and the three pink dogwood trees we planted when we moved in years ago. The home that always looked like a magazine cover at Christmastime with a wreath and a candle in every window. And the holidays—those wonderful family events with the laughter and food and the special times together. Gone! It was all gone!

Standing in that initial impact of the storm, my heart ached and cried out in fear and confusion. What would I do? Where would I go?

At night, I cried myself to sleep, praying that when the new day dawned, it would have been a terrible mistake—a bad dream. But it wasn't a dream. Instead, it was a never-ending storm that hurt so bad I was numb with pain.

And so began the longest and most difficult journey I could ever imagine—a lonely journey to the very core of my being.

There are many books, many writers, many speakers that believe God sends bad things, or God *lets* bad things happen, to test our faith. I, as one believer, have never been able to see that or believe that. God is good and gives perfect gifts.

Because we live in a flawed world, however, bad things sometimes come our way. I am not strong enough to say that I am thankful for dark times, but I can praise the God of all creation for the impact that darkness has had on my life.

Strangely, one of the best things about light is also its counterpoint—*darkness*. These times of tribulation are the places where ideas, emotions, and sensations meet and mingle to bring me into a new awareness of God's light.

So this is a book about experiencing the light of God—sometimes through darkness and sometimes in the glorious good times of life. I do not need to talk you into light—better if I can reveal the radiance of my own walk toward the light.

This book is not a story of grief, or of breaking up, or the loss of a love. Instead it is a book about healing, about becoming whole again after a significant loss, which might be the loss of a job, the death of a loved one, a miscarriage, or any one of the difficult times we all face in life. This book is about living again in God's abundance after a bewildering situation.

You may want to use this book as a daily devotional for the next three months. Along the way in our journey together, I will introduce you to other women who have also conquered difficult times. Stay with me through the journey of the valleys, because I can promise you a full room of illumination at the end of the trip. Together we will celebrate the joy of living in God's abundance.

*But you are a chosen people, a royal priesthood, a holy nation, a people belonging to God, that you may declare the praises of him who called you out of darkness into his wonderful light.*

1 Peter 2:9

*I will give you the treasures of darkness, riches stored in secret places, so that you may know that I am the Lord, the God of Israel, who summons you by name.* —ISAIAH 45:3

If you think that plagues ended when the children of Israel crossed the Red Sea, you have never lived in Middle Tennessee during our cicada plague. Every thirteen years, a rare species of cicada larva make their way out of the ground, attach themselves to the trunk of a tree, sprout wings, and then turn themselves into red-eyed kamikaze nightmares.

During their "coming out" time, the newspapers run stories almost daily on the history of these unusual creatures. Reporters explain that the big, ugly, googley-eyed things are actually blind and only fly toward warmth. Warmth—as in the warmth of *my body.*

If you have never experienced this wonder of creation, you will firmly believe that I have sniffed a little too much Aqua Net hair spray and have embellished the story past truthful proportions. Not so! I am not making this up.

Now first, I will admit to a certain bias against bugs, roaches, and other crawling and/or flying critters. (Well, maybe *phobia* would be a more accurate term.) I am not willing to share space with anything that's little and uses more than two legs. The old promise, "It won't hurt you," doesn't matter a whit to me. I just don't like bugs.

At the time of the plague, I was moving to a new apartment to begin my new life as a single woman. I was leaving my beloved and treasured home, leaving all the memories, and moving to a tiny apartment. It was June, the temperatures were hot, and I was an emotional wreck and physically exhausted. Those unsuspecting cicadas chose that moment in time to crawl up out of the ground. Are you beginning to see a film clip in the making?

Now, in case you missed my point, when I say larva climbed up out of the ground, I am not talking about a *few* bugs. I mean millions, billions, trillions, and bejillions of big, ugly bugs, even by conservative estimates. The trunks of the trees were covered by larva skeletons. The sky was dark with these bug-eyed bandits in flight. The nights were deafening because of their mating calls. The street gutters were clogged with evidence of their short life spans. Pharaoh would have thought he was back in Egypt. No wonder he let Moses and the people go. I would gladly have released anything I owned to have rid us of this plague.

I was moving, moving, moving. Hauling clothes, boxes, china, pillows, paintings. Hundreds of trips from the car into the lobby of my new apartment building, and those blind, red-eyed pilots were bombing me from every direction, attaching their prickly little feet onto my clothing, in my hair, and on my skin.

Each time I struggled inside the safety of that lobby door, I could feel their creepy feet walking up my back, across my neck, and into the wild nest of my hair. Then I would perform yet another version of the Texas Two-Step, adding a lot of flailing arm movements, and using my best Texas language to describe the heritage and the future of that bug. It was impressive!

On one of these trips, Sara was with me. She said

very quietly, "Mother, just calm down. Mother, it's not that bad. Mother, get ahold of yourself!" Then she said very directly, "Mother! If you could just see yourself!" So I stopped and tried to get a mental image of what I looked and sounded like.

I smiled. I giggled. I started laughing. Sara started laughing. We laughed until we were crying. We couldn't stop laughing. And oh, that laughter felt so good! It was fun; it was balancing. It laughed away a thick layer of pain and stress.

I wish I could say that after that moment, I was "all better," and I didn't worry about those bugs again. But that would not be true. I certainly enjoyed that moment. Laughter is, without a doubt, the best healer and the best medicine, both physically and emotionally. If I could package it, or sell it, or store it up for later, I could retire a wealthy woman. But when I do need a good laugh, I just remember the Cicada Two-Step.

I'm so glad that I'll be an older, more mature woman during the next thirteen-year cycle. But I sure hope I'm not trying to move.

*Oh Lord, thank You for a full range of human emotions. It makes life so spicy and interesting. Thank You for tears that cleanse and heal. And thank You most of all for laughter, for a sense of humor, for the ability to see the funny things in life, and for the chance to laugh at myself. What a gift!*

*Only when one is connected to one's own core is one connected to others, I am beginning to discover. And, for me, the core, the inner spring, can best be refound through solitude.*

—ANNE MORROW LINDBERG

The trouble with a journey down into your innermost soul is that you must go alone. This can be very disturbing to friends and family as they watch you disappear beneath the surface of your life.

As I worked through the initial stages of my new single life, I found that some friends were willing to allow me the space and time and privacy I required, but others were not. Some folks were constantly berating me with questions I couldn't and wouldn't answer and solutions I didn't need. Some friends were hurt because they were not the "first to know." Some simply could not understand my need for personal space.

My wonderful and caring adult children were perplexed. The calls kept coming. "Mom, if you are lonely, why don't you come over?"

But I wasn't lonely. I wasn't being rude. I wasn't being psychotic. I just needed time alone with no pressure to talk, to think, or to relate to anyone outside myself. Normally, I am a very extroverted person, but in times of crisis, I need private time to regain my balance. So I entered a time of self-imposed "wilderness exile"—a kind of spiritual coma—during which, I went inside myself.

Spiritual and emotional healing can be much like physical healing of the body. First it takes time; secondly, it needs to happen from the inside out. In times of difficulty, there is just no substitute for time in the wilderness; our Lord taught us that.

It would have been so nice if I could have gone to my great, good place on this earth—in the mountains around Pecos, New Mexico—to think and meditate and heal. But instead, I had to use my imagination and visualize myself there. As my body went about its daily schedule, my spirit was sitting on a mesa in Pecos, searching the depths of my being.

I looked and experienced the deep core of my being. What I found was anger, fear of abandonment, and feelings of loss, hurt, emptiness, and shame. These feelings were profound and intense. They all sat, imbedded in my heart of hearts like giant boulders. And frankly, I was holding on to every one of those big, fierce feelings for dear life. They were painful, but they were familiar. They defined who I was at that time. These feelings had been under construction for a long time, and I felt totally at home with their jagged edges.

But they were heavy! My goodness, I couldn't move. I couldn't breathe with those burdens weighing me down. It seemed to me that I needed to get rid of them. They would just have to go!

In order to rid myself of them, I had to endure a lot of work. *Hard life work.* It would take a lot of effort and a lot of time, but important life work is never instantaneous. For days, in my wilderness exile, I considered that pile of negative, toxic feelings. They were filling the total core of my being, and even though that seemed better than a complete void, there was no room for improvement, no chance for wholeness, with all the sad feelings still hanging on.

My prayers at that time were mostly in the form of silent groanings. I'm glad the Holy Spirit was there to translate. I found that in a wilderness time, you become more receptive and more in tune to God's guidance. So it was not surprising when the message came as clear as a voice—*Release those feelings. Let go! You don't need that toxicity. Surrender what you can't use and don't need. Give up your attachment to anger and fear and hurt. It is familiar, but it's bad . . . and you can live without it. Let go!*

A light bulb went on. It was true; I was holding on to those feelings like a life raft. I made myself a victim, a martyr—it just felt so good to own my misery. It would be hard to let go.

I prayed for guidance. I tried writing down all my hurts on paper. I wrote and wrote about how I felt—the sadness, the pain, and even the anger. And I made a conscious effort to "throw away" my toxic feelings as I crumpled those papers and threw them into the trash.

But those attitudes were powerful and deeply embedded. I had to release them many times over. And my decision to *let go* was a huge step toward healing. After that epiphany, each day became easier; each experience was less painful. I was soon ready for the next step—that of finding the positive, strong parts of myself and restoring balance to my life.

*I will say of the LORD, "He is my refuge and my fortress, my God, in whom I trust."*

*Surely he will save you from the fowler's snare and from the deadly pestilence.*

*He will cover you with his feathers, and under his wings you will find refuge; his faithfulness will be your shield and rampart.*

Psalm 91:2–4

*Deny your weakness, and you will never realize God's strength in you.* —JONI EARECKSON TADA

I had no choice but to simply sit still and restore. My instinct told me to lie low, to process the grief, rid myself of negative energy, and allow enough wilderness time to heal. I have laid myself as bare and empty as I can manage to do.

But if I am going to survive, it is time now to find my way back to the surface of my life. To re-enter the race. To reconnect with the world around me.

I am ready now. The strength to move on is beginning to pool around me. I don't know how or why, but I can feel it coming. I think I can begin the walk toward wholeness.

Now, I am ready to look for building materials, ways to put this mess together again. Finally I can reclaim myself—the person I want to be, the person I was born to be.

I have been embraced by my solitude, tested by the darkness of my soul, emptied of my anger, and cleansed anew with fresh thought. And in this process, I have recovered myself. Wilderness exile has done its job—less of the world has made more of me.

My first act in this positive turn-around is to affirm God as my Great Restorer, who continually brings good out of personal chaos, growth out of pain, and hope out of loss. I praise the God who can take me and create life out of the mess I was. He has blessed me with the courage to get up and to move on at precisely the time I was convinced that my burdens were too heavy. He recreated the very core of my being. He gave me the courage to face reality.

I am now able to celebrate the person He created. I have been gifted with creativity, courage, confidence, compassion, and knowledge of the full presence of God. I have been gifted with a delightful sense of humor, a way of reading between the lines in life, and a good measure of sensitivity for people around me. I make good decisions, and I've learned to let go of things that only pull me down.

I have learned that with God's help, I can—and I will—stand on my own two feet. I have walked through the valley of deep darkness, and now I can move on to the green pastures and still waters. In the depth of my being, I can now feel a stillness, a calm, and a strength.

I am ready to embrace whatever life has to offer. There are good days ahead.

> I will smile more.
> I will continue to pamper myself.
> I will grow more interesting with age.
> I will let go of things I cannot change.
> I will acknowledge my life to be a work in progress.
> I will remember my need to regenerate.
> I will limit the amount of negative vibes in my personal space.
> I will challenge myself to new adventures.
> I will live fully every day.
> I will generate new ideas.
> I will admire myself.
> I will laugh.
> I will raise a flag to me, a woman turned inside out, who survived again.

*But those who hope in the LORD will renew their strength. They will soar on wings like eagles; they will run and not grow weary, they will walk and not be faint.*

Isaiah 40:31

# MEET CHARLOTTE

The illness lasted for several months. By the time the cancer was detected, it was too widespread to control. The doctors did what they could, but Charlotte had to prepare herself for the worst. Her mother was dying. Charlotte was an only child, and her father had died several years earlier. So even though Charlotte had a wonderful husband and three darling children, she had remained close with her mother.

Mother was one of the "backbone" ladies of the church. During bereavement times, she was the one who organized the food for the family. At Christmas, she decorated and helped cook for the church family Christmas dinner. At Easter, she helped decorate the church with dozens of white flowers. Charlotte wouldn't be the only one who was left with a gaping hole in her life.

Charlotte immediately went to her pastor to ask for prayers and support as they all faced those coming weeks and months. It was impossible for her to even fathom trying to get through a day without being able to call her mother when she needed to talk. Mother was a pillar of strength.

When the end came, Charlotte thought her life would be over. But thanks to the support of her husband and children, she made it through, sometimes just one hour at a time—until the day came when she had to go to her mother's house to begin to prepare it for being sold.

Going in Mother's house with the intent of getting rid of things was more than Charlotte could face. Mother had lived in that house for over twenty-five years. Several of the church women offered to help, and Charlotte quickly accepted. The initial plan would be that Charlotte and her husband would go through the house and select the things they wanted to keep. Then the friends would sort through everything else and get it ready for the charity trucks that would come to pick it up.

This plan worked well. Charlotte dragged herself through the house in such a state of grief that she could hardly make decisions. But with her husband's help, she gathered up the jewelry, photos, and other precious items. Then the ladies went to work. They sorted and made separate piles of like items.

In about a week, Charlotte came back to the house to see the work finished, with plans of moving all the items on to places that could use them. But the first pile Charlotte saw as she walked into the kitchen were her mother's special baking pans, the little loaf pans used to make her Christmas bread that she took to all the neighbors. And there were the cookie cutters she used for specific cookies to give the children at church. And there was the big stew pot she used to make chicken soup for folks who were ill or just home from the hospital. Mother had cooked for anyone and everyone who needed a little extra boost—new folks to the church, the preacher's family when they had out-of-town company, and mothers with new babies. Mother's kitchen was a virtual mission outpost.

Charlotte started crying again. *Not Mother's cooking things!* she thought. *They can't go!* "Load those in my car," she told the movers. *I want to pick up where Mother left off. I may not be able to do exactly like she did, or as much as she did. But the tradition Mother started will go on.*

And it did. Charlotte used this way to honor the memory of her beloved mother. She got out Mother's recipe box and she found the chicken soup recipe. She found the special cookie recipe and the bread and the Christmas baking recipes.

It was a marvelous comfort to Charlotte. Every time she pulled out the baking pans, she felt so close to her mother. Instead of feeling tired and worn out with the tasks, she always felt refreshed and renewed. And every time she delivered a dish of food, she told the story of where and how the food was made. And she was careful to remind her children of the importance of carrying on Grannie's tradition of cooking.

*Thank You, good Lord, for helping us find ways to fill our weaknesses with Your ever-present strength and comfort. Help us to see opportunities instead of despair.*

# Seeking God with Your Whole Heart

---

*Call a friend to pray with you. Friendship divides burdens and multiples hope.* —Cheri Fuller

There are so many books on prayer that one could literally make a personal study of nothing but prayer for a solid year, and then there would be new books to read. Even after such a study, true knowledge of prayer may remain a mystery. Prayer is a personal search for God, and it takes on new dimensions from person-to-person and from day-to-day. As we grow, we know more about our contact with God.

Beware of speakers and writers who say they have prayer all figured out. Some will claim that if you follow their "ten steps to a better prayer life," you, too, can become more spiritual. When it's over, what you actually learn is how *they* access God. Of course you can make use of that, but basically, the relationship *you* have with God will follow your own search.

Prayer is simply a matter of the heart—or we could say, a matter of the spirit. It is a matter of *my* spirit getting in touch with *the* Spirit. And, for me, it seems that the connection comes from a burning desire, an overwhelming obsession with finding God.

When the children of Israel were carried into exile and were separated from their beloved Jerusalem, they also felt separated from God. They felt abandoned, displaced, lonely, and far from God's love and care.

Does this sound familiar? It does to me. When the going gets rough and I feel abandoned by the Holy

---

Spirit, I can identify with this lonely, bewildered nation. As I face challenges, and unknown outcomes, I wonder where God is and why I can't hear from Him.

I'm sure the Israelites prayed. I'm sure they worshipped as best they could. But apparently nothing seemed to feel right. They were very discouraged and at a loss as to how they could return to fellowship with God. Then God reassured them through the prophet Jeremiah: "Then you will call upon me and come and pray to me, and I will listen to you. You will seek me and find me when you seek me with all your heart. I will be found by you," declares the LORD, "and will bring you back from captivity" (Jer. 29:12–14a).

Reading this entire twenty-ninth chapter of Jeremiah is such a comfort. And I find my hope in the phrase, *"when you seek me with all your heart."*

Could it be that the worry and distractions of a harried life are causing the static that separates us from God's voice? Could it be that our focus is on a simple and immediate rescue of our own design? "Dear God, let this problem pass from me!" Could it possibly be that we're trying to get a message to Him instead of trying to find His message to us?

If I seek Him with my whole heart, I must first quiet my anxiety. I must find a peace in my heart and life that will leave room for God. I must find rest and clear out the static and interference of the crashing waves. Then, I can focus on God. Jeremiah told the people it would be seventy years before God would release them from exile, so he suggested that they learn how to experience God in their daily lives.

I think the message here is, take your eyes off the trouble and focus on seeking God. Look for Him as a mother would search for her child. Look for Him with your *whole heart*. Look only for God. Accept His timetable. Then God says, *"I will be found by you."*

*Dear Lord, my heart yearns for Your nearness and Your presence. Clear my mind of all the thoughts that are focusing on my plan for deliverance; instead, lead me to Yours.*

*One of the reasons we hold on so tightly to anger
and bitterness is that we're afraid those who've
hurt us will "get away with it" if we let go.*

—THELMA WELLS

*T*he stillness of the evening is unsettling.
I usually have a million things to do. But with my
new pared-down lifestyle and schedule, it emphasizes
the aloneness of my situation.

I look around at my safe-haven rooms, feeling at
home in the surroundings, but feeling uncomfortable
with the fact that no one else is here. There should
be mouths to feed, clothes to wash, cleaning to be
done. In the past, my contrived sense of family was
to give and give and give until I saw satisfaction and
pleasure on everyone's face. Now what? How do I
measure myself now, without those opportunities to
give?

I decided to open family photos and relive the
good times—graduations, holidays, vacations.
Family portraits of the perfect family. A father, a
mother, three interesting kids. Everyone dressed up
for some special occasion. Such happy faces. Fun
times. There is the first college graduation. Surprise
birthday party. Grandmother and Granddaddy coming from Texas for Christmas. My second son packing his new little car for college. Sara's graduation
party. Vacation times in Santa Fe.

Looking back confuses me. The past seems so
real—but so *past!* It is hard to sort through the
starkness of my new life. Looking at the photos, I

wonder, if I had known then what I know now, would I have taken more time to enjoy every little moment in a different way?

A new kind of loneliness engulfs me. But I mentally revisit my cherished home, hoping it will bring me comfort. We had lived hard and loved much in that place. I close my eyes and walk through the front door, remembering how my key fit into the lock. There is the entryway, the stairs, the living room, my kitchen.

On I go, in my mind's eye, through each room, remembering the smells, the colors, the feelings, the happy events that took place there.

Strangely enough, when I do come back to the present, I feel better, soothed somehow. A little visit to the past, on my own terms. Remembering things as I want to remember them, maybe not as they really were. Love gave my life meaning, and the loss of that love would give my life depth.

Now, my mind moves to the future. Oops! Too scary for now. Too vague. Too far away.

For now, I just need to hunker down in this place, in the present time. I need to lie low, process the grief of life lost.

I feel parched, drained, and have no will to go on. Sit still and rest. Cry, if I must. Let the sadness and loss wash over me like high tide. Wash over and move back out to sea. Bend into the pain for now. Because tomorrow is a new day. A time for moving on. A day to see possibilities. A day to breathe deeply of a new beginning.

Oh yes, I want to make this a *new beginning*, not a *sad ending*. I want to be open to new and good and happy times again. But for now, I rest and listen and wait.

*"My grace is sufficient for you, for my power is made perfect in weakness." Therefore I will boast all the more gladly about my weaknesses, so that Christ's power may rest on me. . . . For when I am weak, then I am strong.*

2 Corinthians 12:9, 10b

*How do we take this measure of faith God gives us and make it extraordinary? It's all a matter of focus.* —JONI EARECKSON TADA

*W*e just finished a study of the apostle Paul's missionary journeys. It was an overview of his plans, his commitment, and his ability to move forward in time of trouble.

The study amazed me at one point—when I learned the number of times Paul ran into closed doors. In fact, Paul's life and ministry was more about how he had to traverse barriers than it was about his open doors.

As the study progressed, I was fascinated with how Paul handled the various closed-door situations. He sang. He glorified God. He wrote letters of encouragement. He taught. He just kept right on living his life the best he could despite the circumstances.

I compared Paul's response to how I sometimes handle closed doors. I cry. I fuss. I assume my life is over. I make bad decisions. I whine. I pound on that closed door and conclude I'll never try anything new again.

I wonder why it is so hard to handle an abrupt change in plans. Maybe, for me, it is because I am hardheaded and determined to have things *my* way, in *my* own time. I get a plan in mind, and doggedly pursue that plan, no matter what.

Truly the most difficult moments in life come when those doors slam shut and we are left on the doorsteps, not able to see where to go next.

My friend Amy once faced such a situation. She worked for a specialty retail shop in our town. She had been with the small, locally owned company for six years, and the owners depended on her for every-thing—opening the store early, closing late, making deposits, ordering merchandise. However, after six years, she had received only minimal raises, was not even considered a manager, and basically saw herself going nowhere. The door to a future in gift shop retailing seemed closed. Because of her long work hours, Amy couldn't look for a new job unless she resigned and took a chance that her savings would see her through a job search.

After leaving the gift shop, Amy began by taking a career planning class at the local YWCA. Through testing, she discovered that she would fit well in a social service agency, working with children or spe-cial needs adults. This certainly matched her inter-ests, and it awakened a long-held dream. She believed she clearly felt God's hand in her decision.

Days went by as she applied to a number of agen-cies. The folks at these agencies agreed that Amy seemed to be a fine candidate. They liked her per-sonality and her credentials, but there simply weren't any openings. Funding for new hires was nonexist-ent. Amy took this series of closed doors very seri-ously. She felt confused. She prayed again and again, seeking direction for her life, but five months went by with no job.

During our study of Paul, I was reminded of Amy's job search. Paul tried to follow God's leader-ship, but so often butted into solid, closed doors—sometimes even closed jail doors.

How do we explain this? We pray, we make good choices based on God's will as we see it—and still nothing, no sign, no message. Could these times of uncertainty and confusion signify that God is preparing us for a new stage in our journeys? I don't know, but I do know that waiting patiently for His leadership is one of the most difficult things required of a follower.

Amy finally went to talk to her pastor to see what she was missing in her understanding, or in her commitment. The pastor looked at her with total surprise. "Amy, you will never believe that we have been praying and waiting for someone like you to come." Her pastor explained that a family with a nine-year-old special needs child had recently moved to the church. The parents wanted badly to be a part of an adult Bible study class, but their child needed special assistance to stay in his own church class. If Amy would be willing to work with the family on Sunday mornings, the church could be a significant ministry in their lives.

It was a perfect match, well, almost perfect. Amy was challenged and thrilled at the prospect, except that this was not a paying job; it was a volunteer ministry. But the pastor also knew of a doctor in the congregation who needed a receptionist for his pediatric office, and this job paid very well.

I don't know why it took so long. I don't know why this ideal situation was not immediately obvious to Amy when she first sought God's will. I don't know why God's dedicated people have to face delays, challenges, and sometimes closed doors. But I do know that God doesn't use calendars or watches to mark time. He tells time by eternity.

I know that waiting on God is not wasted time. I know that God is not full of magic tricks that He pulls out upon my command. I know that time helps me focus more on God's priorities than on my personal plans. I know that God loves and wants the best for His children.

I also know that I do not have the mind of God, but I can see His leadership throughout time—from the time of Moses, and David, and Matthew, and Paul and every single day of my own life. I know that sometimes God has to let me run the course of my own ideas before I am ready to hear His plan. I know that I lead a hurry-up life, but God is not a hurry-up God. After all, He has been around for quite awhile.

I think closed doors are a part of real life, but how I handle those closed doors is up to me.

*Dear Lord, clear my vision so that I see opportunities, not closed doors. I feel the confinement of my own closed door right now. Help me look beyond the door and open my heart and mind to Your leadership in Your own time.*

*[The] desert of spiritual despondency was dry and hot and made me oh-so-thirsty for a cup of cold water from the spring of living waters.* —JILL BRISCO

*I* watched a documentary on public television that showed the history of the Roman Empire during the first century. I guess that doesn't sound exactly fascinating, but it caught my attention because I am so interested in the development of the early church. Before Jesus' life was recorded in the Gospels, we have information (recorded in the letters of the New Testament) about how the Christian movement played out in the lives of the early followers. The more I can learn about the ways and the people of that early time, the more I can understand how the life and teachings of Jesus are absorbed and made alive, even today.

Certainly I am no theologian or Bible scholar, but I am an ardent seeker of knowledge. In my own journey I know that the more I can learn about Jesus, the closer our relationship can become. And this is important to me. So I am mentioning these ideas, not because they are new or revolutionary, but because the realization has been meaningful to me in a new way.

As I watched that documentary of Roman life, I realized again that we have so little historical information about the Jewish man from Nazareth. Beyond the recordings in the Gospels, only a small amount of factual documentation on the details of Jesus' life exists.

As I read the gospel accounts of Jesus' teachings, I am struck by how little the disciples seemed to understand about Jesus' message. They tried, but we see instance after instance where they asked the wrong questions, drew the wrong conclusions, fell asleep, acted impulsively, or otherwise demonstrated their lack of comprehension of the big picture. (Much like us today.)

It seems to me that if they had reached a full understanding, then their presence at the Crucifixion would have been more reliable, and their anticipation of the Resurrection would have led them to witness the miracle.

So what eventually transformed the disciples from scared and doubtful men into warriors of the faith who were willing to give their own lives for the cause? For me, that was a pivotal question. If I could discover the secret of their transformation, then I, too, could experience a growing and deepening faith.

Was it the power of the Resurrection? Well, yes, partly. But there had been other resurrections. What gave Jesus' resurrection the impact that changed the world?

As I continue to read through the Gospels and into Acts, I read that another very dramatic event occurred, and with this event, everything seemed to change in the lives of the disciples: the coming of the Holy Spirit. At that point the veil was lifted, and they began to see more clearly.

It seems to me that the resurrection of Jesus, *through the interpretation of the Holy Spirit,* is what gave their lives meaning—and has the opportunity to give *our* lives meaning. The Holy Spirit opened their hearts, opened their spiritual eyes, and enhanced their understanding. And today, the Holy Spirit still defines, explains, and describes God and His purpose in our lives.

The disciples believed in Jesus, or they would not have followed Him. They were good men who tried to be the people Jesus wanted them to be—sometimes understanding bits and pieces, sometimes not quite getting it. But with the coming of the Holy Spirit, they moved from mere *followers* of the Lord into followers who also had transforming *relationships* with Him. Their entire lives were defined by this new relationship.

That is what I want. I want to move beyond just trying to live the good life. I want to move beyond *believing in* Jesus. I want the kind of consuming relationship that makes His ways my ways. I want to take the Christian life seriously.

*And we, who with unveiled faces all reflect the Lord's glory, are being transformed into his likeness with ever-increasing glory, which comes from the Lord, who is the Spirit.*

2 Corinthians 3:18

# VIEWING THE POSSIBILITIES

*What may feel like an end, may be just the darkness before the dawning of a new dream, a new challenge, a new opportunity, a new tomorrow.* —ROBERT SCHULLER

When our daughter, Sara, was born with a debilitating bone condition, it was like taking everything *about* our lives and *in* our lives and tossing it into the air. Some of it came back as problems, some came back as possibilities, and some came back down as opportunities. It was a totally new way of life—a new trip with no road map.

The doctors explained that they only had limited knowledge about *osteogenesis imperfecta*, a physically debilitating condition that causes weak bone structure, and they could give little, if any, support for dealing with the day-to-day care of a child with such fragile bones. Her prognosis ranged from being totally bedridden, because any movement could cause a broken bone, to living with severe limitations because of occasional broken bones.

That blessed emotional pain pill called *shock* numbed our senses for a time, giving us awhile to sort through the possibilities and the limitations. One step at a time, we began to redesign our lives in a way that would be comfortable for every member of the family.

Until that time, I had always worked outside the home. After the boys were born, I dropped back to part-time, but I was out of the house some small part of each day. I made the decision to work because

I knew that I was a much better wife and mother if I had my own work to enjoy. I just loved being with people in the outside world.

We had excellent child care accommodations, and the boys loved going to play school. Best of all, I made just enough money to pay someone to help with the housework, so when we all got home in the afternoons, I could devote all of my time to the children. For us, it worked very well.

But now it seemed that I could not continue my part-time job. Now we had a little china doll who was so fragile that we carried her around on a small padded mattress in our arms. The less we handled her, the less likely it was that she would break a bone. Leaving her with a sitter was out of the question, but we devised a plan for church. We took her to the church nursery and put her in a little crib. The teachers loved her. They told her sweet stories of God's love and sang to her, but they didn't hold her or handle her. My husband, Mancil, or I would stop by between Sunday school and church and check on Sara. At all times, the nursery volunteers knew where to find us.

Many times a day, God and I would talk about how we were progressing, where I needed help, and how we needed to rearrange our plans. Sara had a delightful disposition, and except when she was hurt, she was always sunny. It was easy to devote every hour of every day to that sweet child, but it wasn't long before I realized that I needed to build in some time away. Otherwise, she and I would end up in emotional bondage. She needed to interact with folks outside the family, and I needed to balance my focus in a healthier way.

I hesitantly began to think about going back to work part-time. I didn't know how on earth it would ever be possible. Even the little boys were concerned that I was considering leaving Baby Sara in someone else's care, and frankly, the more I considered the alternative, the more I knew we would have to start looking for miracles. But I knew we would find a way. This was an opportunity, not a problem.

Within a month, I received a call from an acquaintance I had known years before. Out of the clear blue, she called to say that her church wanted to start a weekday preschool program and wanted to talk to me about being the start-up director.

I wonder why we are always so surprised when God sends such direct answers. I barely knew this woman, and I had never even thought about designing and operating a preschool program. But I had the qualifications and experience for the job. We talked, we prayed, and the job became mine. It was a perfect half-day situation. Wonderful church. Nice committee. A match made in heaven.

But there was one *big* question! What would I do with my precious, fragile doll? I couldn't take her to a sitter. No one who knew us would be brave enough to stay with her. We didn't have any relatives within a thousand-mile radius.

I firmly believed then, and believe now, that God does not sit on a throne with a magic wand, zapping down goodies to some people and ignoring others who don't say "please." If that were true, Sara would have been healed in the first place, and we wouldn't even be having this conversation. I believe God gives us strength, wisdom, incentive, and drive to make things happen. And He provides the courage to just keep taking one step, then another step, on the journey. And I think the key is being open to possibilities and opportunities as they come along.

People thought that the job offer was a crazy idea, a dangerous and impossible situation. But God let me see it as a possibility—just the ticket we needed for a more balanced life. I began the search for someone to keep Sara. The boys were in preschool programs, so I needed someone to come to the house, someone with a lot of experience caring for children.

Then came Martha, a little lady who enjoyed working in homes. She met Sara and listened to the special care Sara would need. The two of them bonded immediately. Martha could ride the bus in the mornings, and I could take her home at noon. What a blessing. When I called her references, everyone had wonderful things to say about her. Their kids had all grown up, and they didn't need Martha anymore. So, we became her new family.

Through broken bones, home traction, and the agony of pain, Martha stood by us. She learned to handle Sara as well as we did.

This story shows the importance of *possibility thinking*. Our family faced overwhelming odds in trying to maintain a "normal" family life. It would have been so easy to sit down and let the whole family revolve around Sara and her needs. But, by the grace of God, we knew there was a better way. She didn't need to be the center of the universe, and we didn't need to be revolving satellites. We looked for other possibilities. When we searched with our whole hearts, when we relied on God's leadership, and when we constantly examined possibilities, we sometimes moved forward.

When things work out successfully, it is a glorious feeling. That little preschool that I started over twenty-five years ago is still going strong. Its roots were established in dogged determination and simple faith in a loving God.

*Rejoice in the Lord always. I will say it again: Rejoice! Let your gentleness be evident to all. The Lord is near. Do not be anxious about anything, but in everything, by prayer and petition, with thanksgiving, present your requests to God. And the peace of God, which transcends all understanding, will guard your hearts and your minds in Christ Jesus.*

Philippians 4: 4–7

# ENERGY BOOST

## HOW TO PLAN A
## REALLY GOOD PITY PARTY

*They are most deceived that trusteth most in themselves.* —ELIZABETH I (1533–1603)

*If* experience is the best teacher, then I have learned a few lessons very well. These Energy Boost sections come under the heading "For What It's Worth—Lessons Life Has Taught Me." Now I pass these thoughts on to you, "for what they're worth." May they provide a boost of energy for you today.

How do you plan a really good pity party? We're not talking about a little feeling-sorry-for-yourself deal. Let's plan a superior, hoedown, crying-in-your-milk, world-class pity party. I know how to do this. I've had a few good pity parties for myself, and I've seen a few good pity parties thrown by other people. Here's how to do it:

1. First and foremost, convince yourself that the world *should* be fair, that all the rules should be unbiased and balanced, and that somehow the cards just got stacked against you. For

some unknown reason you have been singled out to receive more than your share of rotten, stinking bad luck. Concentrate on the injustices you have to endure.

2. Think hard about how unlucky you really are. Try to go back in your *distant* past and dredge up two or three examples of how disgusting your luck actually is. No doubt you could find more than two or three examples, but no need. This will be enough to get the tears flowing. It will be enough to make you feel worse than you already do.

3. Berate yourself severely for not being perfect. After all, most people you know *are* perfect, aren't they? Their clothes, their hair, their jobs, their families—all perfect! So, what happened, why can't you just be perfect like everyone else?

4. Replay your negative thinking. This is vital to a *good* pity party. There is no room for positive, uplifting thoughts that could put a stop to a pity party in a big hurry. Continue to focus on what a total loser you are.

5. Stage your pity party late at night when you are already exhausted from the day. If you get a good start on your bad mood just before you go to bed, you can usually stretch the obsessing well into the night, which will make you feel even more tired and worn out. After all, why should you limit a good pity party to just one evening?

6. Serve yourself plenty of refreshments—lots of sugar and chocolate. In the long run, they will

probably cause more problems, so you can have even more parties for yourself.

7. Be sure to stay focused on everything that is wrong with the world as you see it. That will be easy because once you're on a roll, you can think of dozens of bad things.

Well, I hope you're laughing by now because I am being silly and sarcastic. But it helps to look closely at the anatomy of feeling sorry for ourselves.

It's true that life is not fair. Trouble doesn't come in nice measured doses that are evenly divided among every human being. Instead, it piles up on a few people. Everyone is dealt a different hand. But the good news is we all have specific strengths and wisdom for dealing with challenges. Let's seriously consider counterattacks to the big pity party.

1. Develop a compassion for someone other than yourself. Sincerely open your heart to the pain and frustrations of someone else. Sit down and write notes to three people who you know could use a lift or an encouraging word.

2. Practice smiling. I know this sounds really crazy. It is so hard to feel sad with a great big smile on your face, and you'll feel so silly that the pity party will end because you will be laughing at yourself.

3. Plan a surprise for someone who really deserves it—a dinner, a tin of cookies, a pair of tickets to a new movie, a certificate for dessert. There are plenty of people who deserve a good turn, and good turns have a way of multiplying themselves.

4. Name the top five things for which you are thankful. And think of five people for whom you are thankful. (I want to add a disclaimer here: I do not think that pity parties, or downtimes, are a result of not being thankful.) On your back way up, thanksgiving is a good thing.

There is nothing wrong with a little downtime. It happens to everyone. But you need to know how and when to bring it to a close. Bad times and bad moods make you believe that all of life is bad, not just your feelings, and they deplete your energy.

No one is in a good mood all the time. That's not a realistic expectation. But no one should be in a bad mood 100 percent of the time. (That calls for serious consideration.) Bad times and bad moods come and they go. When necessary, treat yourself to a good razzle-dazzle pity party. Then get up, dust yourself off, and get back to your good life.

*Dear Lord, as I read the Bible, I am led to believe that You, too, had "down" times—times when You felt extra concerns and disappointments. Thank You for walking beside me during all kinds of times.*

# OFF BALANCE

*Stress is the response of your mind, emotions, and body to whatever demands are being made upon you.* —STORMIE OMARTIAN

Remember that marvelous old piece of playground equipment—the seesaw? I haven't seen one in years, so I wonder if they have been declared unsafe or otherwise removed from new playgrounds. Seesaws used to be one of my favorites. My propensity for making things even and balanced was right at home on that board as it moved up and down in a nice rhythm when the two participants were evenly matched. It was pleasant, it felt good—sometimes up, sometimes down, sometimes perfectly balanced in the middle.

That is, *if* everyone played fair. There was always the tease who sat on one end of the seesaw and kept you up in the air, feet dangling, for as long as he could manage. I envision this periodically, especially when I am trying to wear too many hats and balance too many jobs. Stuck up in the air, way off balance. And most of it is my own doing. I am a mystery to myself, a person who cannot leave well enough alone. I just keep adding a responsibility on Monday, another job on Tuesday, an obligation on Wednesday, another deadline on Thursday, something fun on Friday, and pretty soon that seesaw is stuck dead still, right up in midair. I'm off balance, again.

Do you also recognize the symptoms of being off balance? For me, off balance means bad headaches, neck aches, being unable to sleep, tiredness, stomachaches—you get the picture. And believe it or not, these symptoms always come as a complete surprise to me. I never realize when I'm packing that seesaw too heavy on one end. Honestly, it sounds like I'm not too bright, doesn't it—continuing to do the same thing over and over, but expecting different results? But my defense is that I love the challenge of juggling several things at once. I love all the things I get involved in, and I'm just way off balance before I even realize it.

Sometimes the little things can add the last weight to the imbalance. I recently had to replace some carpet. When you replace carpet in a small living space, it has a way of totally disrupting life—furniture and clothes everywhere. And, of course, there were delays in the job, so the total mess of my safe space lasted almost eight days. That little episode left me so off balance it took weeks to get that seesaw working properly again.

Sometimes big things can disrupt the balance without warning. You've seen the list many times—the big life-whammies that exert immense influence on your stress levels:

- Death of a spouse or child
- Divorce or separation
- Deep loss
- Moving
- Birth of a baby
- Loss of a job or job change
- Financial loss or bankruptcy

Any *one* of these rates around eighty to one hundred (on a one-hundred-point stress scale) and is guaranteed to knock you totally off balance. These stressors (and others that are not mentioned) are rated high because we have no control over these types of situations. They usually happen without our permission.

So how do you regain balance after big or even small balance problems? There are only two ways: take something *off* one end of the seesaw, or put something heavier *on* the other end. Take a leave of absence from some job or some responsibility over which you you have a bit of control. Let the house responsibilities go. Or work on the other end of the seesaw by adding help—housekeeping help, counseling help, help from friends, and/or nurturing activities for yourself.

Visualize that playground seesaw. Visualize how the weight is stacked on each end; then find a way to shift the load. Being off balance is painful, stressful, and certainly does nothing good for your health. You may not have control over life circumstances, but you do have the power to balance the weight on that seesaw.

*In the pressure of my daily life, Lord, help me to seek balance rather than busyness. Help me to grant myself grace, rest when I need it, and wisdom to set limits.*

*. . . so long as woman labors to second man's endeavors and exalt his sex above her own, her virtues pass unquestioned; but when she dares to demand rights and privileges for herself, her motives, manners, dress, personal appearance, and character are subjects for ridicule and detraction.*

—ELIZABETH CADY STANTON, SOCIAL REFORMER (1815–1902)

$\mathcal{S}$he marched to the beat of her own drummer." I don't know who said that, or wrote or thought that, but I just love it! When all is said and done, and I am no longer on this earth, and a small gathering of friends and relations is sitting around discussing what it was like to have known me, I hope someone is able to remember that phrase and quote it about me. And I hope others in the group all nod and say in agreement, "Well you can say that again! She certainly had her own march and her own tune!"

As an old woman of the tribe, I have the advantage of abundant hindsight. So as I contemplate great lessons learned in this life on earth, I believe that the basic element of personal happiness is *finding the sound of your own drummer and marching to that beat*. The happiest people, the most secure people, the most admired people live by that mantra.

A drumbeat is steady and strong. At a rock concert, the rhythm (and volume) of the percussion can whip a crowd into a frenzy. This is scientifically documented to happen because the constant strong beat of the drums connects with the rhythm of your own heartbeat, and together they just soar. Remember how you can "feel" a parade (bands/drums) as it passes by?

In olden days, armies had drummers who marched into battle with the soldiers. The drumbeat was so loud and strong and clear that the soldiers actually got in rhythm with that beat and marched bravely into battle, sometimes to their own deaths.

In truth, there are no shortages of drumbeats out there. Chances are your mama had a strong drumbeat, and she has likely been trying to get you on her rhythm all your life. (It's just what mamas do.) Your dad may have had his own drumbeat, or he may have chosen to live his life listening to someone else's drum. A strong marriage will have two drummers beating in concert.

Any group, whether it is a club, church, neighborhood, or family, has a bunch of drumbeats. They set up expectations, creeds, and rules that are supposed to determine the rhythm of the group. Words like *should, ought,* and *will* punctuate the language of someone trying to alter your cadence.

Get a red pencil and underline this sentence: *You are at your happiest times when you have found your own drumbeat and can march to it!* Finding your own drumbeat and then giving yourself permission to march to that beat is and will be one of the most freeing and happiest moments of your life. It is when you make your best decisions. It is when you look your healthiest. It is a very empowering time. It means you believe in yourself and are willing to listen to your own song, living in a way that suits you best. As you feel your self in sync with your drumbeat, you draw strength enough to march right into whatever life has to offer.

The trouble comes when your drumbeat has to be

compromised—in a job, in a relationship, in a friendship. These are the folks who hate their jobs, who are exhausted at the end of the day. These people are miserable in their marriages.

It is so tiring and debilitating trying to match your heartbeat with the wrong cadence. I can tell immediately when a task is out of sync with my drumbeat. My heart literally starts fluttering, my neck muscles tighten up (as I try to bring some control to the situation), and in a short time, I have a splitting headache. Almost every time I can trace the feelings back to a situation that threatened my "drumbeat."

For example, I work for a private, nonprofit agency that offers services to senior citizens. Funding for our social service programs is a constant challenge. I feel that our agency is a top-notch, expertly run organization. We can stretch a dollar farther than anyone and can offer services for thousands of homebound seniors with the smallest budget. But this takes people power—both staff and volunteers.

Our funding sources often have to make rules and regulations for the distribution of their money. Sometimes these guidelines grow and grow, and we have to jump through hoops of mega proportions just to get a tiny bit of money. So instead of offering services to people who desperately need help, we spend our time dancing on the head of a pin to get a few dollars.

This process just about shuts me down completely. So what do I do? I try to recognize these situations of breaking cadence, and then I finish my work and live in the situation until I can move back to my center. Then I evaluate—is *most* of my life and/or job and/or relationships a matter of compromise on my part? Or are these the *rare* occasions with *most* of my life/job/relationships working in beautiful harmony?

Do you see what I'm saying? In short, *be yourself!* Be around people who are happy with who you are, and who are not constantly trying to change you.

See yourself as a blank sheet of music with the time signature (drum cadence) already set. God did that part. Now you can write the melody, but it needs to fit into your personalized way of doing things. The fulfilled life will only support your true personal song.

> *I praise you because I am fearfully and wonderfully made; your works are wonderful, I know that full well.*
>
> Psalm 139:14

*Don't get too sophisticated to be frequently amazed.* —Victoria Moran

The power of both positive and negative influences in our lives never ceases to amaze me. Our days and hours are like big sponges soaking up either happy, pleasant feelings or mean, negative feelings. And the results of either are quickly obvious.

Last Thursday I got home from work and felt so happy and energized. As I contemplated my happy mood, I became curious about what caused it. I mentally traced my day back through the different events to locate where those happy feelings were coming from. Oh yeah, it was that meeting with Beverly. She and I work so well together. We create good programs, we laugh a lot, and we enjoy the process. But it is more than that. More than just being with a fun person. Beverly gives off plus signs; she sprinkles "happy dust" wherever she goes. When I'm with her, I immediately feel good and my mood shifts to a higher plane. She sees humor in things that could be mundane. She is confident and knows her ideas are good ones. Beverly is just a sincerely *plus* person.

With little effort, I also can think of folks who give off minus signs. Those folks you just hate to see coming, but you can't really put your finger on why. The person who can make a negative statement about *any* situation.

I can think of an outstanding one right off the bat. One summer, I was traveling on a speaking tour with a person who could turn sugar into salt, and did so with every sentence. I would say, "Look at that beautiful yard with that wonderful landscaping. I love the way they arranged the flowers." She would reply, "Yeah, it makes my back hurt just to look at it."

I'd say, "We really had a nice time tonight. The people were so responsive, I could have gone on for another twenty minutes." She'd reply, "Yeah, except for that rude man on the back row. I didn't like him one bit."

That woman could suck the life right out of any moment. She dropped minus signs in every direction. Spending time with minus people wears you down. It's hard on morale for everyone in the group.

My point is: It is important to surround ourselves with plus people! And it is just as important to develop a strategy for dealing with minus folks. One week I tried to focus on people and/or experiences that brought pluses or minuses into my life. Every time I encountered a plus person or a plus experience, I made a mental note. I immediately became aware of the amount of good vibes that entered my personal space. These were the events or people who enriched, encouraged, and promoted good, positive feelings.

I also kept a mental tabulation of the minus people and events that invaded my territory. These were the times that made me tired, that wore me down and sapped my energy.

At the end of the day, I tabulated the results. No matter how hard I worked, or how long my day was, if the pluses far outnumbered the minuses, I felt less tired and less stressed. Conversely, a few significant minus encounters left me exhausted at the end of the day.

Now the real surprise here is that I can add my own plus marks to my day. If I give off pluses to others, it empowers me in an emphatic way. As I move from encounter to encounter encouraging others with kind words, giving positive input to friends and coworkers, I actually create plus feelings for myself.

Positive surroundings are healthy—a positive outlook, a sincere interest in other people, positive interactions. It is important to your physical self to promote the happiness that keeps your body healthy and your immune system functioning. Without plus feedback, you will wither.

Very negative vibes are like people pollution. Minuses affect your blood pressure, your digestive system, and your respiratory rate. Remember how hard it is to take a deep breath when you are listening to negative talk or incessant complaining.

And this just might be a good time to double-check the number of pluses and minuses you contribute to others, to the office, to your family, and to your friendships.

The point here is to identify where the negative impulses are entering your space, then limit your exposure. And keep a close check on your positive input. Now that I have been aware of this for awhile, I can begin to tell when I feel seriously depleted on the plus contributions. I can work much better if I stop and find someone to laugh with, visit with, or somehow create a *plus rush*.

Your body needs food, and your spirit needs pluses.

*Dear Lord, how thankful I am for the happy, fun, positive people You bring into my life. Sometimes*

*I am a little prone to focus on results, on getting the job done, and forget all about enjoying the journey. Thank You for the people who bring a smile to my face and a good feeling to my day.*

# THE FAMILY LIVES ON

*Crises can bring unity or division, growth or decline as a family, progression or regression, closeness to God or alienation from Him.*

—KAREN DOCKREY

*C*hase is our family stabilizer. Firstborn children tend to be responsible, accountable, and driven by a certain feeling of family obligation. Even with these duty-bound attributes, Chase loves life like a twelve year old—canoeing, rollerblading, skiing, rock climbing, and hiking. When he and his wife and children recently moved to a new home, it took ten large cartons just to move all his play gear.

Chase has always been a type of surrogate parent to his younger siblings—much to their chagrin. He felt it was his duty. We all depend on Chase in a thousand ways—and he responds with willingness. During our family transition, Chase supported, strengthened, and surrounded each of us with steadfastness and calmness.

What benedictions are given to children by their family roles! From earliest childhood, roles are chosen for members of the family: caretaker, the family clown, the frail one, the crazy one, the loving one—roles that the family both sees and enforces. It seems to me that Chase was the out-front man. He had been offered the role of strength and stability. I think at times Chase suffered under the tiring burden of being the brother everyone looked up to—drafted as he was into the ranks of leadership. The cool one under siege. I've never really known if strength was his gift or his act—perhaps it was a little of both. But it worked. The firstborn son, forever that.

Whatever Chase's standing in the family was, he now has eclipsed his personal specialties by marrying Melanie, and the two of them have given us Abigail and Baby Evelyn—gifts of love to our entire family. Now he can revel in the role of father, that responsible role he knows so well.

As Chase and Melanie move beyond their families of origin to carry on the centuries-old tradition of creating their own family, I desperately search for my magic wand to make their paths straight and pain-free. So far, I'm not able to come up with guarantees. But what I *can* give them is space to love and live as they see best, support to undergird their hopes and dreams, and the most sincere intercessory prayer I can offer for God to give them strength to meet their challenges.

Maintaining a marriage and raising children are two of life's aggregate tasks, the Alpha and Omega of venture. It will time and again test the metal they're made of, but with these two young parents, I see perseverance, stamina, optimism, and an unceasing commitment to the job.

Watching their little family take shape is like a big dose of past, present, and future; brief glimpses of how things *used to be* in our family with small children, the delight of seeing it reenacted *now*, and the great dreams we all enjoy for the *future* of those little girls.

How I love families, even with all the warts and bumps. It is still the best way to live on earth.

*I will sing of the LORD's great love forever; with my mouth I will make your faithfulness known through all generations.*

Psalm 89:1

*God has been where you are going—there's nothing to fear. God has been where you've been—there's nothing to hold on to, all is forgiven.*

—LARRY KEEFAUVER

Of all the friendly, outgoing, glowing women I have encountered, Margaret stood out like a beacon, always spreading her happy nature to church friends, neighbors, and the hospital corridors she visited each week. But that all changed one sad Friday.

Margaret and her beloved husband, Stan, enjoyed fifty-one years of married life, before Margaret had to say good-bye as her childhood sweetheart succumbed to a long bout with cancer.

The illness had been draining, and both Margaret and Stan agreed that death would be sweet compared to the pain and suffering they each experienced—Stan as he lingered helplessly and Margaret as she had to watch his decline.

But as Margaret followed the hearse to the cemetery and watched the casket lowered into the cold, gaping ground, she felt a crushing pain beyond her wildest nightmares. Death was not sweet—it was horrible!

How? And why? Retirement had been absolutely delicious—full of travel, friends, speaking engagements, enjoying the grandkids. Life just didn't get any better. And then that dreaded diagnosis! Now she was alone.

As Margaret went through the motions of each day, she lost her flow. She couldn't even find happiness in seeing her precious grandchildren. Being with them was more of a chore than a pleasure. Until one day, when her daughter called with an urgent need for nine-year-old Robert to come and stay for a few hours, and Margaret reluctantly agreed.

Robert, with his tousled hair, arrived with a bag of his own toys and games since he knew Granny's house was no longer a happy place to visit. He was a good little boy and amused himself quite nicely for a while. Margaret acted busy with some insignificant house chores so she wouldn't have to talk. But finally, Robert began following his granny around, and expectantly opened a conversation, "Granny, where is Papa?"

The question stung hard, and Margaret felt a tendency to double over with pain. She looked down at Robert's precious little face, with his big brown eyes intently locked on her own.

"Robert," she replied, barely above a whisper, "you know Papa is with God now."

"Why does that make you so sad? I think being with God is a good thing."

Margaret was momentarily without words. "Well, I guess it is a good thing. I'm sad because I miss him so much. I need him here with me."

Robert thought about this for a few moments, and then said, "Well Granny, you got me. I make you happy, don't I?"

Margaret reached out and drew Robert to her in a big hug. His warm little arms circled around her waist and he held on tight.

In that instant something came alive inside her, an indescribable warmth like standing in a soft summer rain. She remembered a verse, "And a little child shall lead them . . ."

What followed was an afternoon of remembering, talking of good times, going through old photos, even getting out Papa's fishing rod and remembering those special trips to the lake.

All at once Margaret realized that a big part of Stan *was* still with her. Stan's presence and his spirit was everywhere. And this tiny child, who had opened the windows to her soul, was the breath of Stan's breath and the pulse of Stan's heart. Still here with her!

How could she have missed so great a gift? Reaching out to life, touching life, remembering life, brought a peace that she had not felt in months—a sense of security, a feeling of connection that reached across the abyss of death. A comfort that began to sustain her on a daily basis. A little child had led her.

*O good and generous God of the universe, thank You for the wisdom we enjoy from the minds of children. Surely their faith is most like the simple faith You want us to have. May we trust You in the same beautiful way that a child trusts You.*

*To rely on God's power, you must acknowledge your weakness and seek the strength only He can give.* —CYNTHIA HEALD

$\mathcal{R}$arely is any event so bad that there isn't a sliver of silver lining hidden in the experience. Ours was no exception. Our family structure was changing, the beautiful home was gone, the family was scattered. But our loss in this situation was Sara's gain. It was like the crash broke open a wonderful seed that just began to grow and flourish in the most exciting way.

While we were in fruit basket turnover mode in terms of living arrangements, Sara spoke forcibly, "It's time now. I want my own place." The family looked at her in wonder, knowing that when Sara declares something, Sara makes it happen. But the odds of her being able to live on her own seemed unrealistic.

Sara uses a wheelchair and sometimes a wheeled walker for mobility. But from day one, what she lacked in physical aplomb, she made up for in spunk and determination. Sara's bones break easily and an ill-placed bump or hit can result in a broken leg, arm, or collarbone, many weeks in huge body casts, and weeks of rehab. So her life has been a big breath-holding balance between keeping her "safe" and allowing her the freedom she needed and wanted.

When she was younger, she frequently made references to what *her* house would look like, when she had her own kitchen, the colors she wanted to use in decorating. How that would happen, I could never have guessed, but I encouraged the dream. Sara's life would be full enough of barriers, without my taking her dreams away too. So we fantasized about Sara's house while the rest of the family looked at us in doubt. However, we each knew that if Sara decided it would be so, it was so!

So it was no surprise when she invited me to go with her to see a condo. She had researched the possibilities and found a high-rise condominium building where some of her friends lived. The entire building was totally accessible, with big rooms to accommodate a wheelchair, big windows to let in lots of light, wonderful views—and it was close to her work, just exactly right for her in every way.

But how on earth could it work?

So many times we had been at this exact juncture. Too scared to move forward, but too fearful to hold back. We lived with risk on a daily basis.

Even as a child, Sara was bright, happy, and adventuresome. Consistently confining her would have only served to break her vitality and make her dull and dependent, but allowing her to go and enjoy life to the fullest was constantly risking pain and unbelievable suffering for her and the whole family.

How did we get through? Very carefully and by the grace of God! We tried to take educated risks and go to the furthest limits we could stand. Many, many times Sara would make the decision to even extend beyond the first limit. But I truthfully say, it was always the best thing. Sara made good decisions and went beyond every goal she set—piano lessons when she couldn't even reach the pedals, rollerskating parties in a wheelchair, public schools, and college (magna cum laude), a graduate degree, and a career where she gives back to the system that supported her.

So now, Sara says she's moving out on her own. I don't say, "No way!" Instead I say, "I don't know how we're going to do it, but let's take it one step at a time and give it a try."

Sara confidently assures me, "It *will* work!" And it did.

Sara became the proud owner of her own condo, which is decorated just like she said it would be and is the scene of many a Bible study group, prayer group, church party, sleepover, group meal, and whatever folks can do together to have fun. There is always an assortment of interesting people and interesting activities taking place at Sara's home.

There couldn't be a prouder, happier homeowner on earth. That's the other part of the silver lining in the story—when the odds are way against you, and you succeed anyway, it is so sweet!

*If any of you lacks wisdom, she should ask God, who gives generously to all without finding fault, and it will be given to her. But when she asks, she must believe and not doubt, because she who doubts is like a wave of the sea, blown and tossed by the wind.*

Paraphrased from James 1:5–6

*It is easy to be like the Pharisees in thinking that if we work hard and try to be perfect, then God will accept us.* —Cynthia Heald

There ought to be a better word to describe "making a big change." I'm talking about *risk*, but that word calls up visions of a flashing red light. I looked in the thesaurus to see if I could find an alternate word, but it only got worse: *dangerous element, possibility of loss, specified hazard, danger, peril.* Goodness, can't anyone say anything good about *risk*? No wonder *most* people lead lives with little or no risk involved.

Let's rewrite a definition for *risk* as it applies to life circumstances. Now, for the record, I'm not talking about bungee jumping here, or going on a rattlesnake hunt. I'm talking about making a change in your life direction. Let's use less dangerous-sounding words like *speculation, gamble, leap in the dark, plunge, venture, chance.*

There, that sounds better, doesn't it? Of course, any way you look at risk, one part of the meaning is the same—*unclear outcome.*

Playing it safe in any decision rarely allows growth or challenge or change. That old saying from the women's movement back in the 60s reminds us, "If you always do what you've always done, then you'll always have what you've always had." Or another version that I heard recently says, "Insanity is doing the same old thing, in the same old way, and expecting different results."

Basically, I do not have a problem with folks who are not very good at risk-taking—as long as your life is one big happy cream puff. If your relationships are all intact and functioning within 90 percent of full potential, if all of your satellite persons (children, parents, in-laws) are speaking to you and to each other, if your income and vocational goals are right on, then good for you! Give me a call because you are one of an endangered species.

But in the lives of the rest of us, there are times when change is definitely necessary. It will require you to climb out of your comfort zone and make a decision to change, even when the outcome of that decision is unknown. That's *risk*. And that's what initiates growth.

I think there are at least three things that keep us from giving risk a chance. The first is *old habits* or *comfort zones*. These are like an old pair of house shoes. I have my favorite old pair. They're comfortable, and they're right there waiting on me when I come home from work. I can't even wear them to the garbage room because they look so bad. But I've had them for so long, I don't feel right getting rid of them. What if I can't find any that feel as good? So I just won't bother looking. See what I mean?

Probably the biggest reason people avoid risk is fear of failure. Somehow, the word *failure* sounds even worse than risk. *Failure!* Doesn't that just cause your heart to skip a beat? It's like a threat of doom—something to be avoided at all costs.

*Hey, I've learned it's okay to fail!* Everybody does it—everyday. Hardly anything worth doing turns out 100 percent successful every time. I am a huge football fan, and I watch my team run up and down that field, trying to kill each other in order to make a touchdown. For two hours this madness goes on. And on average, except for a few plays of the game, they *fail*. It's part of the game. But the fact that they risk life and limb is what makes it a game worth my screaming my lungs out. Risk is the heart of the game.

The third reason folks shun risk is that they want to hold on to what's familiar. In our city, the YWCA runs a shelter for abused women. When I worked there, I was able to get a close-up view of what battered women endure. It's not pretty—but for many of them, it is familiar. Sometimes the woman feels more secure holding on to a familiar life situation than reaching into the unknown for a different life. Of course, for a battered woman, this risk can be truly a dangerous and life-threatening risk. But you get the point. Status quo can be a comfortable spot when compared to moving out into the unknown.

*When* should one take a risk?

- If a part of your life is holding you captive and not allowing you to move on to full maturity and potential.

- If your old habits are self-destructive.

- If you are living with chronic stress and unhappiness.

- If you experience stress-related physical symptoms.

- If you are being battered, either physically, emotionally, or in any other way.

- If you are stuck on a dead-end street and your life is going nowhere.

- If you would like to see a change in yourself.

> *How* do you take a risk?
> Well, you can close your eyes and jump!
> Or you can do your homework.
> Explore the various possibilities.
> Give the idea time to gel.
> Make another plan if necessary.
> Talk the idea over with someone whose
>     opinion counts.
> Then take a calculated risk. And once
>     you decide to move ahead, don't turn
>     back!

I can tell you that risk is hard. I never enter into a risk situation lightly. It takes a great deal of courage. But sometimes it is as necessary as breathing. Practice risk-taking on smaller life choices so that you can see how it feels. Allow your children to take calculated risks; this teaches courage and decision-making skills. Consider risk and failure to be a part of life and change and growing, not something to be mourned and dreaded.

And above all, never underestimate the goodness of God. He will not leave you or forsake you.

*"For I know the plans I have for you," declares the LORD, "plans to prosper you and not to harm you, plans to give you hope and a future. Then you will call upon me and come and pray to me, and I will listen to you. You will seek me and find me when you seek me with all your heart. I will be found by you," declares the LORD.*

Jeremiah 29:11–14a

# My Great, Good Place

I've heard writers and speakers extol the virtues of visiting the ocean for times of retreat, focus, and meditation. It's one of those places you go to find balance. In fact, I've heard folks describe many venues of comfort and tranquility—places that are special, very private in selection, and vastly important to folks who are privileged to find solace there.

So let me take you to *my* great, good place on earth. The place where I can most easily see God, feel God's presence, and just bask in the knowledge of God—Pecos, New Mexico.

For years of my adult life, I have returned there again and again to experience joy, alleviation from anxiety, and the mercies of God's goodness. Through the cycles of my life—as a high school student, as a college student, as a young adult making career choices, as a young married woman beginning a new life, as a young mother with big responsibilities, as a mature woman experiencing the pleasures of midlife—I found myself, for all too brief days, back in my great, good place. Throughout these life cycles, my soul came to rest, surrounded by the indescribable beauty of those New Mexico mountains.

I know that there are more beautiful spots—higher, grander mountains, maybe more picturesque streams and valleys. But for *me*, there is something about that Pecos spot that *connects* with the deepest vein of my existence.

For one thing, there is so much history all around. For thousands of years, other inhabitants walked on that same land. The remnants of churches and villages endure to remind us that men and women stood on that spot centuries ago, seeking God. The fact that they felt dependent on God, and sought Him with all sincerity, clearly connects me to them.

At a particular spot on a mesa, as you stand in the courtyard of an ancient place of worship, you can see over fifty miles in every direction, 360 degrees. The sky is so big and usually pure crystal blue. The mountains are majestic and powerful, reminding me of the vastness of God's everlasting mercy. For generations, men and women just like me stood in that spot and *knew* God. That realization always gives me goosebumps. At that moment, I am connected to the Divine, to ancient humanity, and to all of nature. I feel complete and in perfect balance with God in a way that I cannot feel in any other place. The only thing missing is a triumphant pipe organ to reverberate music off the surrounding cliffs. Instead you have the gentle songs of the birds.

And the wind! The wind is so special there. I have been there in storms, which is a profound experience. You easily can envision God sounding the thunder drums and setting the lightning in place in a grand display of affection for the earth. But on clearer days, the most wonderful wind plays around your body like gentle hugs and caresses. And I know that it is the same wind that touched the Native Americans before me. I always think of Jesus' conversation with Nicodemus. "The wind blows wherever it pleases. You hear its sound, but you cannot tell where it comes from or where it is going. So it is with everyone born of the Spirit" (John 3:8).

Members of my family often joined us in New Mexico during summer visits, all the cousins enjoying being together. One year, I wanted them to see my great, good place, so we all made the small hike out to the ruins. Daddy had a very difficult time walking the short distance out to the mesa. It would be his last visit and our last family time with him, although we didn't know it at the time. He died of heart disease in the next few months. I'll never forget the effort he made to visit my great, good place.

During another year, my sister and her family joined us again in New Mexico. We decided to drive deep into Holy Ghost Canyon for a picnic. The drive is breathtakingly beautiful. It feels like you just shed layer after layer of care and worry as you drive along, and by the time you are well into the canyon, you are free and relaxed. We laughed, we played in the ice-cold water of the mountain stream, and we built a little campfire to cook our food and give us warmth from the chilly air. It was the most marvelous, simply *fun* time—memorable in every way. We have photos that show our happy, relaxed, contented faces.

Soon after that marvelous day, my precious sister was diagnosed with the breast cancer that eventually took her from us. That time with her in my cherished canyon was the nicest memory ever. How I thank God for that day in my great, good place.

I know that God can be experienced anywhere, anytime. For that I am grateful. But my daily walk with Him is so much sweeter when I remember how it feels to be with Him in my great, good place.

*Dear Lord, I am most grateful for our daily walk together, but I am also most thankful for our special times in the beautiful spot where I feel Your presence in such a unique way. Your Spirit comes to me, as it did to the generations of seekers before me, through the vastness of Your creation. When my will is weak and my resolve is weary, renew my strength with thoughts of that great, good place.*

# ENERGY BOOST

## FOCUSING

*It is the small doubts of tired souls that accomplish their ruin. It is the narrow vision, the fear and trembling hesitation, that constitute defeat.*

—ALICE FOOTE MacDOUGALL (1867–1945)

Everyone needs a place they can go to empty the pain. A place where you can refocus and reclaim strength for living. There are at least a million ways to do this, and you often see magazine articles and books describing various meditation techniques that promise everything from healing to wealth. I can't comment on these other processes, but I know what works for me.

My quiet, contemplative time re-centers my attention on God. It is an important process to me because I can be high-strung and prone to a quick temper. I tend to manufacture stress. Friends and family have often laughed and said, if I ever started to unwind, I would twist myself into the floor!

I can be impatient with myself and others, and I constantly overschedule my time. Maybe because of these characteristics, I have developed health problems that result in constant chronic pain—sometimes debilitating pain. In addition, watching Sara manage her chronic, daily pain saps my energy. And in my job at the senior center, I deal with a wide variety of people, deadlines, and financial concerns. These are the facts of my life: what I live in, with, and around.

It is easy for me to fall into a trap of making these circumstances and concerns the primary focus of my life—then I constantly obsess about the trouble. That is where my re-centering comes in. It is all about *refocusing*.

Sometimes I have to close my office door and just sit still for awhile. Sometimes I find a quiet place at home. I sit in a comfortable chair, close my eyes, and remain still for as long as I can spare. Just sitting and breathing in big, deep, relaxing breaths. That, in itself, is very calming. And the calmness gently leads you into a feeling of openness and hope.

As I am refocusing, I try to do four things.

1. I face the life circumstances I am in, and I acknowledge that a constant focus on these situations is draining, painful, and depriving me of strength. I list all these things to myself and "breathe" them *out* in some of my deep breaths. This helps me to empty all of the pain.

2. I look for anything else I can get rid of. Sometimes in haste, or a weak moment, I pick up problems, or misunderstandings, or conflicts that actually belong to someone else. If I look carefully, a few peripheral thorns can be eliminated, passed on, delegated, or scratched off my

list. I cull the superfluous, keeping only what I need.

3. I gently move my focus off the painful and onto the strength and peace that is available to me from the Lord. I focus on God and His strength, which can be *my* strength, when I claim it.

4. Then, I rest in the green pastures and beside the still waters that the Lord has provided for me.

This is not easy, I assure you, but this process will help you reclaim the power and the peace that have been robbed from you by life situations. When you are centered, you are in touch with God at the core of your being. Only then will you feel balanced, peaceful, and clear about your life.

*O good God of mercy, thank You for helping me re-center myself, and in the process, making me more available to Your power and to Your peace. You are always there for me; it is I who wander off into the maze of the calendar, with each entry on the schedule moving me farther and farther from the gentle water and green pastures that I seek. Thank You for helping me find the way back to Your care.*

# A Feather, a Rock, and a Pebble

*To do good things in the world, first you must know who you are and what gives meaning to your life.* —PAULA P. BROWNLEE

*I* first discovered my refocusing process in my great, good place in New Mexico. One summer I was feeling a big burden of responsibility and needed time to regroup and rethink, so I took advantage of the extravagant scenery and started on a long walk. Along the way, I found and collected three items that have become the tools I use in my centering process, time and again. Now I am describing how I use those items so that you can apply it to your life in a way that might help you.

My walk through a path in the canyon started by just clearing my mind of everything I could as I went along. I wanted to focus completely on God's creation around me. I was trying to soak up some of that beauty so I could pull it out when I got home. But I found much more than the splendor of nature.

I first concentrated on the big sky. The air in New Mexico is so clear and crisp that the sky just seems more blue than the blue in Tennessee. It is beautiful, freeing. The white fluffy clouds play through the vastness of that sky. For a long time, I watched a large bird almost floating through the air a short distance away. I imagined myself floating with that bird— effortlessly riding the currents of air, finding the breezes. I guessed it was a large hawk. The wingspan was impressive as it glided so peacefully above the frays of life, weightless and without care. The more I watched, the more my neck and shoulders relaxed, and the worries started to fall away. I don't know how long I flew with that bird, but it made an indelible impression. I kept repeating the verse from Isaiah 40:31: "But those who hope in the LORD will renew their strength. They will soar on wings like eagles; they will run and not grow weary, they will walk and not be faint."

As I continued my walk, I found a feather on the path and picked it up to remind me of this special moment.

Next, I focused on the magnificent mountains. It is easy to think of strength and shelter in the rock, and the majesty of an all-powerful God when you are standing so small before those great mountains. The ridges are jagged, the mesas are restful, the changing colors are fascinating.

Another of my favorite verses came to mind, "The LORD is my rock, my fortress and my deliverer; my God is my rock, in whom I take refuge, my shield and the horn of my salvation" (2 Sam. 22:2–3a).

The process of focusing on those mountains and their symbolism empowered my tired spirit; I realized that the strength I needed was at hand and was mine for the taking. I found a small, jagged rock on the path and added it to my pocket with the feather.

My third focus led me to the rushing waters of the mountain stream. I noticed how the water washed over the rocks. I noticed how clear and refreshing the water was. It quickly carried away a tiny stick I threw in the current.

Our church choir had recently presented a beautiful anthem based on a wonderful verse from Isaiah. I remembered the music and the verse as I watched that water: "When you pass through the waters, I will be with you; and when you pass through the rivers, they will not sweep over you" (Isa. 43:2).

I found a little pebble that the water had rounded over the years and added it to my collection.

As I thought about my life and the challenges I was facing, I felt the hand of God on my shoulder, and together we looked at the three treasures—a feather, a rock, and a pebble. It all added up to grace. God's grace was sufficient for this day and the next and the next.

I carried those items home and still have them in a fancy little box. At first I took them out frequently, one at a time, and revisited that walk when I needed centering time. Now I don't have to look; the items and their messages are locked in my mind.

*My Maker and Creator, thank You for showing Your love in so many ways. Thank You for promises both seen and read.*

*I must release my imagination from self-imposed, limited, too small thinking.* —ROBERT SCHULLER

The fall of the year is usually goal-setting time for businesses and agencies. Employees sit down individually, then come together in a small group, then a larger group. They decide specifically what they want to accomplish in the coming year.

It is tedious work. The employees look at last year's goals to determine how successful the company has been, and then they either expand those goals or close them out as completed. And if you want to look good, to look like a team player, you'd better come up with a few new ideas to work on for the next year.

This is a quiet, computer-time activity, which involves some heavy-duty thinking. All of these things tend to border on "ho hum" to me. I'd rather be involved in a people activity, but I can clearly see the necessity of the task. If we don't set goals, we can just about kiss progress good-bye. Business, industry, and even nonprofit work have realized this for years.

In recent years, my agency added two new columns to our goals and objectives: "Who Is Responsible?" and "Time to be Completed." So now, not only do I have to set the goals, I have to either take personal responsibility for each one or delegate responsibility (which means I still will be ultimately responsible). On top of that, I have to say exactly how long it will take me (or the assigned person) to accomplish the task. My hide is really put on the line when I do that!

At the end of six months, if I haven't increased my numbers by 5 percent, we look to see who was responsible for the assignment. Sometimes I see that there is no one to blame but me—I was responsible for that goal.

I liked it better when I could say, "Well, it really wasn't my fault. The numbers just didn't fall in like they should have." Or I could blame the staff: "They just didn't work hard enough," or "Times are bad, and it affected our growth." As long as I can blame someone or something else, I am off the hook.

Can you see where I am going with this? That's right, the importance of *personal* goals and objectives. Hey, it's not a bad idea! Get a pencil and paper, or open a new file on your computer. It is time to create your personal goals and objectives.

This is *not* the same as setting New Year's resolutions. New Year's resolutions are usually doomed to failure from the beginning. They are frequently unrealistic—more like "dream-on" philosophies than anything else. True goals and objectives are solid strategies that are based on realistic plans to get you where you want to be. They can be, and should be, stated in microsteps so that you are sure to experience some success along the way.

If you have a hard time getting started with personal goals, ask yourself, "What is working for me right now?" Or "What part of my life is on track, heading in the direction I want? Do I need to set any goals to insure and perpetuate this good direction?"

Then ask, "What in my life isn't working so well? What is making my life miserable?" You guessed it! You need to write a goal to make the change.

Now comes the biggest and most important part of this whole process. Filling in the *"Who's Responsible"* column. And who do you think is responsible for all the growth and all the change I want? My mother? My brother? The lottery? Publisher's Clearing House? I wish! No, girlfriend, it is me—me, and only me. I need not look to the right or the left. And no need to phone home. I need to write my own name in the responsibility column.

What about the time column? How long will it take me to meet my goal? Set the date.

Do you see what happens here? When I assume full responsibility for my own growth and development, my own happiness, I can make things happen for myself. I have a right to an empowered and productive life. I have within myself the resources and the energy I need to begin. I have gifts and possibilities enough to achieve anything I want. I am the one charting the flow.

Then when I meet my goals, I celebrate, I dance, and I sing. I congratulate myself and plan a nice reward for myself. Setting and completing personal goals is a sign of strength and commitment to myself. A big thumbs up!

*I know what it is to be in need, and I know what it is to have plenty. I have learned the secret of being content in any and every situation, whether well fed or hungry, whether living in plenty or in want. I can do everything through him who gives me strength.*

Philippians 4:12–13

# NUMBER TWO CHILD

*Disabilities and illnesses are not gifts for special families or rewards for strong faith. They are results of living in this imperfect world—distortions of God's good.* —KAREN DOCKREY

Isn't it amazing how three children can be raised in the same home, by the same parents, and yet present in such totally different ways? And isn't it always surprising how birth order makes such a tremendous impact on personality?

I have been conducting an unofficial survey (one that is highly influenced by what I already believe to be true) on second-born children. It seems to me that first-born children tend to be the "do-right daddies" of the family, and second-born children have a higher measure of personal independence. By third- and fourth-born children, you just get a nice combination of all of it. Everyone is so used to babies by then that they just love them and never worry about their personalities.

Our second-born son, Jason, is a treasure trove of high spirit, creativity, intelligence, and big-time persuasiveness. In other words, he is a salesman of epic proportions. At age one, he stood up and simply addressed the world with authority and confidence.

Jason is also an addicted risk-taker. He is at his finest when he is living on the edge, scaring himself and everyone else. The mundane simply bores him to death. It comes as no surprise that he was a "kindergarten drop-out"—he came home one day and declared, "That teacher taught me all she knew on the first day, so I don't need to go back!" Jason preferred learning "on the wing," so to speak, instead of sitting still and listening.

These characteristics drive the education system crazy—and they should. Our schools tend to lose their brightest students because they insist on only one method of teaching—sitting down and listening. But that's another soap box.

Jason and I share many of the same core values: freedom of the spirit, fairness for all, and a tendency to think outside the box. I totally admire the courage he gathers on a daily basis to pursue these values to their limit.

But the virtues that have been Jason's most conspicuous are his uncanny intuitive powers and his sensitivity to the pain of others. He redefines empathy. As Sara's big brother, he considered it his role to defend, delight, and befriend her. He beat the daylights out of kids who dared cross Sara at school. He challenged teachers to their face, if he felt them to be unfair to her. He carefully coached her little legs to take steps again after broken bones healed. He constantly taught her about bugs and critters, machines and football, and other important life lessons.

Because of their closeness, Jason is in agony when he watches his little sister suffer. Her incidents with broken bones seem like experiences from the third circle of hell—the emergency rooms, unfamiliar doctors, pain, and surgery. Her pain is Jason's worst nightmare. But it is Jason whom she wants most to see during the days of recovery; no other member of the family can cheer Sara or ease her pain like he can.

Families are such enchanting gifts—all the different kinds of people coming together in one household. I've sometimes thought it was like eating my delicious sour cream pound cake. If you ate the ingredients separately, they taste awful—can you imagine trying to down a cup of flour, or three raw eggs? But when you mix them all together and bake it awhile, every ingredient has a chemical reaction with the other, and the result just "melts in your mouth," as we say in the South.

You take your children as they come. We can't make any special orders. But Jason would have been my special order. He is the spice in our cake.

*But Mary treasured up all these things and pondered them in her heart.*

Luke 2:19

# MEET LOUISE

*W*hen you think of fun, vitality, spunk, and elegance, you have just described Louise. She is a ballroom dance instructor, a talented needleworker, and an active member of her church. If you want something done, and done well, contact Louise. If you want to see poetry in motion, watch Louise on the dance floor.

So when *macular degeneration* (a degenerative spot on the retina resulting in blindness) struck her, the blow was tremendous. Within eight month's time, Louise's sight was almost gone. It was a loss of devastating proportions. None of us could conceive of Louise with such a profound disability, and Louise was furious. She called me one day and demanded I do something immediately! "I'm going blind by the day! I need help. Please help me."

Louise wanted to lash out at any person she could get on the phone line. Her two daughters came from Florida and Atlanta to help make "arrangements." Their plan was to quickly put Mama Louise in assisted-living accommodations where she could be cared for safely and securely. But what they hadn't reckoned with was Mama's fighting spirit. Louise would not move and would not listen to any arguments of such a plan.

Louise had been in the same house for over twenty

years. It was in a well-kept, older neighborhood around friends she knew and loved. To get her out of that house would have taken a fight that could have made newspaper headlines.

The girls reasoned, begged, and explained the circumstances over and over again. But Louise dug in: "Just leave me alone," she said. "I'll think of something."

They had no choice. Social worker after social worker came to the house to talk to Louise. But Louise would listen to none of their conversations. She was mad, and she was scared. The loss of her sight and her independence all at one time lit a fire inside of her that gave her strength and determination well beyond what she had ever demonstrated before.

Today, as she and I look back, we realize what a healthy thing this anger was for Louise. It helped her work through so many of the negative feelings of despair, pain, and loss. But it was a difficult experience for her girls. They had wanted to act quickly to put Mama in a safe place, but finally, in exhaustion and exasperation, they went home to their own families. They decided they would let Mama stew for a few weeks and come to the realization on her own that she needed help. They knew that the loss of sight would leave Louise vulnerable and alone, and she would come to her senses eventually.

Again the girls misjudged the fire in their mother's tenacity. For a few more days Louise sat, basically cursing the darkness, hating her new life of dependency. She continued to make phone calls to various agencies and individuals, jumping on people with claws extended.

As I tried to work with Louise, I realized she would need to get the anger out before we could make any progress in establishing help for her. I prayed that she would use that anger only as a stepping-stone to more constructive expressions.

One day Louise called me crying. "I'm so sorry," she said. "I have been rude, but I'm scared. I don't know what's going to happen to me. What should I do?"

At that point we finally were ready to go to work together in a healthy, productive way. First, we called Connie, a vision specialist who visited Louise in her home. The specialist confirmed the diagnosis with the doctor and then went to work. Connie rearranged a few things in Louise's house and began to teach Louise the fine art of living in a dim gray-and-black world.

Within a few visits, Louise was able to turn her anger into coping skills. Her creativity and intelligence started working for her, and between visits from Connie, Louise devised plans and adaptations for herself. She became more and more excited about how she could maintain herself in her own home with some help from a home visitor.

Louise happily discovered she could still go dancing. With a partner, the dance floor was still a fun and accommodating place. She worked with the physical therapist at a local exercise club and found great release in keeping herself physically active and fit.

Her daughters were astounded. First one would visit, then the other, to see this miracle that had come to pass. One of them helped Louise enter the world of computers. We found a volunteer who went into her home, set up her new equipment, and installed software for vision-impaired users. Sure enough, in no time at all, Louise was using her computer to become a familiar name to her legislators, reminding them often of the need for services to persons with vision loss.

Could Louise have adapted to her new disability in an easier way? I doubt it. A loss as profound as Louise encountered is a shock; it is unfathomable. I think Louise was well within reason to fight the circumstances with every ounce of her being.

How wonderful for her and for all around her when Louise started taking responsibility for her own outcome. It was not smooth sailing from that point on by any means. She still cannot get to where she needs to go at a moment's notice. She has to wait for rides to the grocery. Many things still need to be worked out. But Louise reports that as long as she can measure the great success she has had in most areas, she can maintain a degree of patience for other problems.

I tell Louise's story because it is such an exciting example of a person in dire need, who simply stood up, made a plan, and went to work to make a bad situation better. I am so proud of what she's done.

*Thank You, dear Lord, for strength and companionship in times of trouble. I am thankful for Louise and others like her, who face insurmountable odds, yet find the strength to move beyond, reminding us yet again that Your grace is sufficient.*

---

*Let the little children come to me, and do not hinder them, for the kingdom of heaven belongs to such as these.* —MATTHEW 19:14

On a trip to Washington, D.C., in 1988, I accidentally happened on a kiosk entrance to the Smithsonian. Like Alice in Wonderland, I followed the stairs down to a new International Gallery and found the most spectacular exhibit I have ever experienced in all my museum wanderings. The hundreds of artifacts from worldwide sources focused on how families around the globe and across the centuries have rested their hopes in the promise of the new generations.

The photos showed how parents and extended families face the birth of new babies. I was spellbound with the emerging images depicting how cultures welcome their newest members; how a family communicates the hardship or the joy of the new baby.

I have been fascinated for years by a newborn baby's profound understanding and uncanny ability to absorb messages from the new world. This exhibit both expanded and confirmed my understandings.

Some babies are born into immediate privilege—their birth alone destines them to be kings or queens. The child represents status, proof of fertility. In other cultures, even sometimes within our own country, the birth of a baby represents nothing but another hardship, another mouth to feed, with scant provisions already stretched thin. The little one's presence strains an already crowded home. A wretched destiny.

---

Some babies are separated from their mothers at birth and cared for by substitute parents. Surprisingly these are the more privileged births. Other cultures, sometimes the most primitive and ancient cultures, make specific provisions to attach the baby to the mother with little portable cradles or carriers or pouches. The mother and baby are never far from each other for the first years of the baby's life. Think of the bonding, the rich love that these two share forever.

Some cultures feel a child should not be handled so often, should be left alone to cope with the world as best he can—being fed at prescribed intervals, on schedule. Other babies are born into caring hands and soft voices that are first lessons of their family's love.

How a culture welcomes their newest members says more about the people than any history book ever written could. Whether a baby is born in a modern hospital, in a mud hut, in a warm bed, or under God's open sky, the first moments of that birth mark the pattern of the culture on that child.

My seniors and I recently attended a Mother's Day celebration at a Hindu temple. The program consisted of the adorable Indian children performing dances from their culture. The children were wonderful. They were dressed in elaborate clothing that had been imported from India. Even the tiniest children had beautiful bracelets on their wrists and ankles. Their creamy brown skin was the texture of soft velvet. Their big brown eyes simply twinkled with excitement and mystery. We were enchanted as we watched these gorgeous children twirl and turn and use the graceful hand movements of the dances.

But even more charming was watching the members of that culture take such pleasure in their children. Except for the few of us, the audience consisted of extended families and friends. Those parents and grandparents hugged and encouraged them and talked about how beautiful they were. Those little dancers got so much nurture during that evening, it was joyful to watch.

What a different world this would be if much funding, focus, and training could go into making it a good place for all newborns and young children. If we put a collective effort to the support of maternal–infant bonding and nurturing, so much would change for the better.

*People were also bringing babies to Jesus to have him touch them. When the disciples saw this, they rebuked them. But Jesus called the children to him and said, "Let the little children come to me, and do not hinder them, for the kingdom of God belongs to such as these."*

Luke 18:15–16

*Praise the Lord, O my soul; all my inmost being, praise his holy name.* —PSALM 103:1

Welcome baby girl, you are now one of us. With the help of God, we will do our best to nurture you and protect you. We will love you, hold you, and teach you. We will enrich your days as you will embellish ours.

Thank You, God, for Your unspeakable gift. I will know Your love when I look into the face of this beautiful child. I will know the sound of Your voice when I hear her little sounds. I will know the warmth of Your care when I hold her close to my heart. Oh Lord, You must love us so much to have sent such a precious gift.

Blessings on your life, Sweet Baby. May God expand your love to cover the earth in your sweetness. As you love and are loved, you will know God. Welcome, Baby, to a world that has been waiting for you and for all that you will be and bring. The very fact of your birth stirs our love and we receive you with open arms. Welcome.

Birth Blessing for Mary Abigail Ezell
March 31, 1999

I stood at the nursery window and watched the exuberant yells of my first grandchild. Tears were streaming down my face. My prayer of thanksgiving was so far beyond words that all I could do was experience the overwhelming emotion. The birth of a new baby simply stands as the most monumental miracle in all of mankind.

Now God had given us Abigail—a beautiful little

child, carrying my genes into the future, connecting all of my past to all of her future. It was nothing short of breathtaking. This tiny child holds the promise of continuity. She will be a likeness of all of us and yet none of us. She will be her own person, unique in every way, her own contribution to our family and to our age.

Standing in that hospital corridor at that moment, I could never have imagined the sheer joy, the fun, the total absorption I would have with her. How could one tiny hand holding on to mine, lead to so much happiness?

# NEW BABY EVELYN

*I will sing to the Lord all my life; I will sing praise to my God as long as I live. May my meditation be pleasing to him, as I rejoice in the Lord.* —PSALM 104:33–34

*H*ow could this be? Another little gift? Another grandbaby? Our joy was beyond measure. How could we be so blessed?

*Who are you, tiny child, sent from God? What have you brought us? Laughter? Talents of music or dance? An understanding of numbers or science? Will you have your mother's chin or your dad's eyes? Will you teach us a new zest for life and show us a new way of looking at the world? Who will you be, tiny child? Will you heal broken spirits with the kindness of your words or quiet storms with your calmness?*

*I am curious about all we don't know yet. How will you present? Will you be outgoing or shy and demure? Will you have to run double steps to keep up with your big sister's fast pace?*

*Who will you be, sweet baby? I know. You will be all that God meant you to be. You will give to the earth all that God sent you to give. And I will be there for you, Sweet Baby Evelyn, giving you all my unconditional love, playing tea party with the bears and dolls, singing fun songs, and making the best memories we can design. Blessings on you, sweet baby. Blessing on us all.*

*Birth Blessing for Evelyn Lucas Ezell*
*June 13, 2001*

This baby has the advantage of coming into a home of experienced, loving parents. Her big sister helped train Mommy and Daddy and set the stage for years of security, consistency, and jovial good times. Such excellent parenting, one rarely sees.

Abigail and I were housemates while Mommy and Daddy were at the hospital getting Evelyn born. We had a tea party, we ate lunch, we went to the art gallery where Abigail selected a big googley frog from the gift shop to take to new Baby Evelyn. Then, the ever-feminine Abigail selected some dress-up clothes to wear for the special occasion—a big lace collar and a significant strand of long pearls. Finally, Sara, Abigail, and I, all with our carefully selected gifts, went to the hospital to welcome our newest member.

The ecstasy of walking in the door of that room, holding the little hand of one of God's most precious gifts, then peering over the crib to welcome the new baby—it just doesn't get any better. All the extended family was present and taking full joy in the event. We passed the new little bundle around for everyone to hold and welcome in their own ways. The pastor came and we had prayer. The simple astonishment of that moment was like standing on holy ground. Now I am more convinced than ever, heaven is all around us; you don't have to die to get there. Welcome, Evelyn.

*You can never live anyone else's life, not even your child's. The influence you exert is through your own life, and what you've become yourself.*

—ELEANOR ROOSEVELT

We started out with Abigail riding in her stroller. But as we moved through the shopping mall, the lure of beautiful colors and various wares overcame the joy of riding, and we abandoned wheels in favor of walking. Eighteen-month-old Abigail and her Mimi, hand in hand, through the mall.

Her lack of knowledge, as yet, about the plan of purchasing everything in sight saved us a lot of heartache as we just meandered around, enjoying the hustle and bustle.

Soon we decided that an ice-cream break was in order. So we got a big scoop of vanilla ice cream and settled down for a feast. One bite for Mimi, one bite for Abigail. It was sheer delight watching that little-bird mouth open again and again for a bite of that extra delicious ice cream. That simple day will always be in my memory as one of our best bonding times.

I have very strong feelings about being a grandmother. I took parenting very seriously, too, but I took it *too* seriously, thus losing much of the fun because I was so intent on doing it *right*. The responsibility just weighted me down. But now, I have no need to *parent* these sweet babies. They have their own Mommy and Daddy. And these two young parents are doing such an expert job, they don't need me to chime in on the parenting; I am just totally free to supply the grandparenting. In other words, I don't need to bake the cake; I just supply the icing.

In my opinion, grandparents are essential. Whether near or far, this basic relationship is vital to a child.

*Grandparents provide unconditional love and acceptance.* They are always there to love and accept and encourage. I had a grandmother like that, and my kids had a grandmother like that too.

Mama Dear was my anchor, my private cheering section. She loved me without reservation; even when I was unlovely, she still thought I was wonderful. Her house was a place of safety and security for me, full of treasures that she let me play with because I was more important to her than things. She made me beautiful clothes and bought me surprises.

My mother was the same kind of grandmother to my children. She loved without reserve. They went to her in times of trouble and need. They relied on her acceptance and her opinion. She played with Barbies on Sara's hospital beds for hours. She cheered for the good times and wept at the sad times. I want to be that kind of grandmother—solid, caring, strong, and supportive.

*Grandparents connect children to their past and to their roots.* I have started making copies of old family photos for the girls. As soon as they are old enough, we will take out the family Bible that dates back to 1850 and holds the names, dates, and pictures of our ancestors. Maybe someday they will be interested in the details of the many family members who came before, but for now, Abigail loves to look at the solemn faces and strange clothing.

Abigail and Evelyn were christened in a dress that has been handed down through the years in Melanie's family. It is a special way of saying, "You are a part of a larger whole."

I am helping Abigail to journal her own history. Until she is old enough to tell and write her own versions of life experiences, I am writing down the events she would be too young to remember later in life. There is a journal of stories to give her when she is much older, and there is a storybook with loose-leaf plastic pockets. I write a story about something she and I did; then I illustrate the story with photos. Abigail reads the story over and over again. I can see the wheels turning as she remembers each part of the event. There is room in the book to add stories as we go along. (Which reminds me, I need to get to the store and start the book for Evelyn.)

*Grandparents teach by modeling what we want children to remember about life.* Good times, happy times, how to get through bad times, ways to be true to yourself. So much about God and living a life in His presence doesn't have to be put into words. It certainly doesn't have to be preached. It can simply be lived, and grandparents do that very well.

I think grandparents need to support parents in every way. Parenting is not always easy, and there can always be questions and doubts, such as "Are we doing this right?" Support, support, support.

I also think it is important to obey their rules. On this point, I need to fudge on the truth just a little. The rule in Abigail's house is "no cookies before supper." Weeeellll, sometimes at Mimi's house we do have just a little bit of cookie sorta in late afternoon. But we confess our wrongdoing right away, and Mommy says, "That's okay, just this one time."

Aside from small bits of cookie, however, I think parents should make the rules, and grandparents should uphold the parents in these decisions. This teaches respect—if Mimi thinks Daddy's rules are important now, Abigail will grow in understanding of guidelines and limits as they get harder to live with during teenage years. I feel it is a big mistake to undermine the word of the parent.

How I pray that my part in this grand process points the way to God's eternal love and purpose. I am not just passing through, enjoying the ride; I am committed to digging deep—creating and recognizing moments of everlasting significance. I am seeing in these children my own limitless future.

*Dear Lord, help me as a grandparent to love and support as You love and support. Help me to be the strength, when their strength runs low. Help me to be wise and caring, knowing that I can make this a happier time or a nightmarish time. Help me to always add to the joy, not ever to the hurt. Help me to live always in the shadow of Your love, so they will know exactly where to find me.*

# SING, MIMI, SING, ONE MORE TIME

*Oh, little baby, who will sing you a lullaby?
Who will sing you gently to sleep? Who will
send you into dreamland with sugar plums and all
good things? Well, me, of course I'll sing to
you—soft lullabies, funny happy songs, music of the
universe, songs that teach, and songs from my past.
We will sing together, little ones—you and I.*

—SUZANNE DALE EZELL

Abigail and Evelyn both think their Mimi can sing very well. They don't mind if the pitch is right (or wrong) or if the notes all blend (or if they don't). They just like the time we spend together, rocking and singing. They like the words—it doesn't matter if they are nonsense rhymes or babies crashing out of trees on broken limbs.

One night Abigail and I got caught driving in a terrible storm with blinding sheets of rain and strong winds. How did we handle the apprehension? By singing, of course. "Baa, Baa, Black Sheep"; "The Alphabet Song"; "Twinkle, Twinkle Little Star"; and "Pitter Patter, Down Comes the Rain"—over and over and over. As the wind blew and the car rocked, Abigail requested tune after tune—"Sing, Mimi, sing, one more time," she would say.

When we finally arrived at her house, her anxious parents (who had *not* been singing) met us at the door. Abigail poured out the whole story in one breath: "There was a BIG storm and Mimi sang loud, and we weren't scared." What a vision that little child is going to carry into her older years—driving through a storm, with Mimi fiercely gripping the steering wheel of that little beetle bug car, leaning into the windshield, trying to see through the rain, belting out verse after verse, "ABCDEFGHIJKLMNOP!"

Now that Evelyn is here, we three will make such happy music together. The Bible never really says that angels sing. It refers to the host of birth angels as "praising God," but believe me, when my sweet babies and I sing our fun songs, angels are in chorus!

*My heart leaps for joy and I will give thanks to him in song.*

Psalm 28:7b

# A Bucket of Prayer

*Prayer is not helping God with an answer; it is asking God for help.* —Becky Tirabassi

In the novel *The Prince of Tides*, author Pat Conroy describes a funeral parlor smelling of "dead flowers and unanswered prayers." Within the context of the story, the phrase accurately describes the conditions of the characters in the story. In the context of my life, the phrase sent me on yet another personal tangent, thinking about prayer and the answers we require.

From my earliest church experiences, I heard lesson after stilted lesson on how God answers prayer— "yes," "no," and "maybe." Then the teacher stood in front of us with a pious, smug look, feeling that he had just revealed a profound understanding of prayer. The people who believe that this is the sum total experience of prayer are the same people who likely will be standing at the death scenes of friends and family with nothing but "no" answers, or "un"-answered prayers.

Easy answers are limiting because once we receive an easy answer, we tend to sit down and call off the search for more understanding. When we pray, using mostly prayers of petition, and then wait for responses of "yes," "no," or "maybe," our knowledge of God is *too small*. We are going to the well with a teaspoon instead of a bucket; Sometimes, we want our expectation to become God's mission.

Volumes of books and writings have been written on understanding prayer. I have only scratched the surface and am barely beginning to put together a working plan of communicating with the great God of the universe. It is an awesome and fearful experience.

Prayer is a personal and private thing, so I cannot set forth a plan that will fit everyone. What I say here is strictly a personal testimony of how prayer works in my life. I am a seeker and a follower, not a scholar. Take what you will and move forward to find your own dimensions for being with God.

First, I believe that prayer is a process of entering into a relationship with Almighty God. It is how we attend to and nurture that relationship.

As an oversimplified example, let me say that I see prayer somewhat like a mother-and-young-child relationship. I love watching Mommy Melanie working with two-year-old Abigail. Abigail knows a lot of words but is still primitive in her expression. The two of them, however, are so in tune with each other that words are not even necessary. Melanie *knows* what Abigail needs and wants. She antici-pates hunger, fatigue, temperature, needs, and desires. The two of them are together in thinking. Lots of what they "say" to each other goes well beyond the limits of language.

In some rudimentary way, this is a glimpse into prayer: God and me, spending time together and just knowing each other, building our relationship. Sometimes we "talk" about what is on my mind and heart, what I'm dealing with in my life. There is also a lot of thinking time, still time, and listening time. My spiritual language, too, is simple at best. So, it is with thanksgiving that I realize prayer is a matter of *being* in the presence of God.

Sometimes I use a simple sentence to connect to the Spirit and shut out the busyness around me, such as "Lord Jesus Christ, Son of God, have mercy!" Those may be the only words used during that prayer encounter. This is far from the "shopping list" prayer many of us say. The one where we present our wants to an outside superparent with the expectation the list will be returned with little check marks next to the items we are approved to receive that week and little "x"s by the "no" items. Some items are left blank, making us wonder if these are prayers that fall into the "unanswered," "ignored," or "not in his will" categories.

Of course, one of the perils in this kind of prayer is that the outcome may be different from the one we requested; then we assume that God did not answer our prayer. We are far more concerned with the *answer* than we are with the prayer. Thus, like the statement from the novel explains, funeral homes would be filled with unanswered prayers.

True prayer understands that pain and death are a built-in part of life. God does not make life a bed of roses for some followers while leaving others to experience despair and loneliness. Move beyond those alternatives. Move into oneness with God. Expect His comfort and power to be with you in good times and in bad times. Expect God to know your heart and expect Him to bestow His fullest blessings on you, regardless of life circumstances. God's love will surround you and give you peace. All our other needs and wants pale in comparison to that. Can you imagine having the strength and peace and understanding to deal with all of life's big whammies?

Prayer is a way for us to connect with God's plan. It is not about figuring a way to get God into our plan. In a "seeker prayer," you and God are moving in the same direction—wanting what is best for you. Prayer opens our hearts to the reality of the sacred.

Lay down your market lists of wants. Lay down your teaspoon. Then go, through prayer, to the well of God's love with the biggest container you can find.

*Dear God of infinite grace, who has called me into eternal glory, make me strong, make me firm, make me steadfast in prayer.*

*Our prayers do not provide information for God.*
—Cynthia Heald

So then, for what should we pray? And what about intercessory prayer? And prayers of healing? Do they "work"?

I believe that God works with what God has to work with. God works with the world as it is and works to bring it to what it can be. God works within the realm of nature as He set it into motion. Prayer does not eliminate suffering or our mortality. Death is a part of life, and it will continue to be so. And as much as we dread and worry, illness and pain can often be a precursor to death. Our bodies are mortal, they have flawed parts that wear out, give way, and become diseased.

If God stepped in and altered the course of nature every time we prayed for wellness, this world would be in chaos. The stark reality is that our lives on earth are greatly influenced by the frailties of the human body. With the pollution, dangerous highways, and deadly superbacteria in the world today, it may seem a wonder any of us have lived healthy lives at all.

So, with this in mind, how do we pray?

If prayer healed all people, my sister would still be alive and among us. My dad would be here, and also my grandmother. If prayers healed, my sweet Sara would be walking and running anywhere she wanted to go, no longer needing her wheelchair. And she would never have had to endure the agony and suffering she has faced from so many broken bones.

Does that mean I don't believe in miracles? Does that mean I will not pray for a better life for Sara, or my mom, or the very sick husband of my friend?

Prayer is a great and wonderful privilege. It is the way I come to know God's love. God believes in me and is constantly working for my good and for the good of all my children. But I cannot use the ritual of prayer to try to control the pain and storms of life. I must turn loose of my desires and expectations and accept the circumstances in which I live. I must move from expecting that God will protect me from the reality and hurts of life to a state of a fuller understanding of life in Him. For example, God may bless me with perseverance to get up when I fall. And each time I fall under the burden of my cares, I am again lifted to a fuller life. That is a miracle!

So, I pray for miracles. That God will take the scattered and fragmented pieces of an illness, of a setback, of a break up, of a loss, and weave these pieces into a stronger fabric for the journey. I pray for the creativity and power to bring life out of loss, to make possibilities out of pain.

God doesn't take away the pain of living or dying, but He can help you face the pain and loss head-on and then walk with you as you transition to a new kind of wholeness. That's a miracle! And for me, that's the result of intercessory prayer.

Pray! Pray for yourself. Pray for others. Pray often. Ask for blessings. Expect great things from God. But *release* those prayers into God's will. Give up your desire to control and manipulate the outcomes of your prayers. Look for transformation, not answers.

Always, and again I say, always remember God's unfailing goodness to meet us where we are, and together we will work for our good. God is the source of ever-present hope and empowerment. Trust Him to know the outcomes.

*To the God of hope, the God of all possibilities, and the God of goodness, walk with me into the future You have planned, using the strength only You can supply.*

# ENERGY BOOST

## MAKE A NEW PLAN

*Do not worry about tomorrow, for tomorrow will worry about itself. Each day has enough trouble of its own.* —MATTHEW 6:34

I love to win—an argument, a game, a planned project, you name it. I just love to win. I expect to win and to be successful in most things I undertake. Now, to be very honest, I am not always totally successful; of course, no one is. I just said I *like* it when I do succeed.

Part of succeeding, or winning, at most any project is to make a plan that will achieve the results you want. Whether I am working on an assignment, a problem, or an event, I try to make a sequential, step-by-step procedure, which breaks the project into small segments. I grab a pencil and paper and literally start with step one.

But as you might guess, even this is no guarantee for success every time. Sometimes I make a plan and execute it to perfection, but things still don't turn out as I had hoped.

Not enough people came to the fundraiser.
The paint all ran together on the furniture
I was refinishing.
The theme party flopped.
That friend still won't speak to me.
The meeting in which I asked for a raise
was a disaster.
Now I am faced with a losing situation, not
a winning one. So I need to regroup.

Contrary to my first thought, I have to realize there's nothing wrong with me. I'm not a flop or a failure or a disaster. I just need a new plan. Plan A didn't work to achieve the results I needed, so I simply need to move on to Plan B, or C, or even D. Whatever it takes to get me where I want to be.

Take heart! Thomas Edison failed dozens of times. The headmaster of his school warned, "He will never make a success of anything." His father called him a dunce.

Albert Einstein was such a failure in high school that one teacher encouraged him to drop out. He eventually failed the entrance exam to the Polytechnic Institute.

It took Winston Churchill three tries to pass the entrance exams to Sandhurst.

Highly successful people succeed only because they are not afraid to try a new plan and give problems a second, third, or fourth shot.

Before moving on, however, I recommend taking a minute to analyze where Plan A went wrong. Why didn't the first plan work? On careful examination I have discovered several reasons why I often have to move from busted Plan A to a second try.

1. *Was the first plan totally realistic?* Magazines and newspapers often print glorious stories of people who achieve superhuman results by bulldozing their way through a series of obstacles. But these true stories are few and far between—that's what makes them news stories. For the most part, sticking to more realistic goals achieves more positive results.

Don't read me wrong here. I'm certainly not suggesting that you never tackle challenges with spectacular, super-duper firework plans. Far from it. I applaud risk-taking. People who never take risks miss a lot in life. But high risks are exactly that—they risk a belly-up outcome.

2. *Did I jump in too fast?* Would more thought or more planning have served any purpose? Sometimes you can even wait a problem out and a solution gently falls into place. Again, a risk. I always resort to my Kenny Rogers plan: "You gotta know when to hold 'em, and know when to fold 'em." And I might add his words, *"when to run."*

3. *Did I get all the facts?* This point is made clear to me almost every day at the senior center where I spend my working hours. Occasionally, a senior citizen or staff person storms into my office with a drastic story of how she or he was wronged and how I must rush out and correct this personal abuse on the spot! I have found that when I react immediately and try to right the wrong, I often am stopped in my tracks with the other half of the story—the new set of

facts changed the total picture drastically. Now my policy is to let any problem simmer on the back burner for a few hours or days until I'm sure I have all the facts.

4. *Is the problem bigger than I am?* Would input from an outside source offer a better perspective? Without a doubt, some problems are just beyond my coping ability; I may be too emotionally involved. A sane, detached person can frequently zero in on some aspect of the problem that will be just the insight I need to make a new plan.

Thank goodness, the general population is moving beyond the stigma of asking for help. Seeking counsel and input from professionals is a sign of wisdom and strength, not of weakness.

5. *Was I creative?* I've often heard women say, "What choice did I have? I just had to . . . ." At first glance, it may seem like you only have one course of action. But think again, is that one action based on how you've always done things? Or is it what your mother would have wanted you to do? Think through everything one more time. There might be a new thought, a new creative solution for your Plan B. As they say in the business world, "Think outside the box."

Now, when Plan A folds and leaves you with an unresolved problem, evaluate whether you were realistic, check your timing, assess your fact finding, consider your need for help, and apply creativity.

Then move ahead with total personal confidence to Plan B, C, or D.

This reasoning, by the way, worked great with our children. In the midst of perceived failure and frustration, I would sit down with a tense, pent-up child and suggest that he make a new plan. I was careful not to take the problem as my own, and not to offer too many suggestions, but to only serve as a sounding board for young minds to think through the facts once more.

*Dear Lord, sometimes I get so overwhelmed with problems and responsibilities, I wonder how I can get through the day. So many people depend on me and the decisions I make that I feel a heavy responsibility to always "do the right thing." Please help me make good decisions, based on Your guidance and care. And when I need to start over again, help me see new paths and new possibilities.*

*We never can tell how our lives may work to the account of the general good, and we are not wise enough to know if we have fulfilled our mission or not.* —ELLEN HENRIETTA SWALLOW RICHARDS (1842–1911)

 As we go through life we build up sets of assumptions that eventually become the mantra that determine our courses of action. We use these sets of assumptions to make decisions.

These assumptions begin early in life, many of which are handed to us by well-meaning adults. Do you recognize either of these?

"Don't do that; you'll fall and hurt yourself."
(Implied message: don't take risks.)

"Don't go out in the rain; you'll catch cold."
(Implied message: don't test your limits.)

Because these statements come from the wise adults in our lives, we assume that they are true. Even if we dared to go beyond these "rules," we would become so burdened with guilt that we would sabotage the experience, or we would have such a miserable time, it would hardly be worth the effort.

Early on, the art of risk-taking is nipped in the bud. As children, our choices were eliminated, and implied failure was pronounced.

Let's take the "walk in the rain" question. The first option is to walk in the rain, get cold and wet, ruin your shoes, and return home to the negative "I told you so." If you get sick anytime in the next six months, it will be blamed on the walk in the rain. Even if you don't get sick, the judgment of "bad choice" hangs, unspoken, in the air.

The second option is to stay in the house and miss out on the rain. So sad! A walk in the gentle spring rain is so much fun; it just opens a whole new world. You can't go through life missing walks in the rain.

Two options and two negatives. What a shame! But what if I refuse to accept those two options? Do we always have to stick to an either/or decision? What about a simple third option? What if we put on rain boots and a poncho and got an umbrella, then took a walk in the rain? No adverse reaction!

See how easy that is? *Oh sure, that one is easy,* you say. *We're just talking about a walk in the rain.*

But it works for big situations too. People with independent, free spirits learn to use this method repeatedly to get past big hurdles. One of my specific hurdles took place when I went to college.

Back in the "olden days," college offered limited options for female students—elementary education, nursing, secretarial science, and home economics about covered it. (In today's world, I know this is hard to believe, but it is true.) So I started college following the largest crowd—elementary education.

By my second year, I knew my days were numbered. One more of those dull education classes (I hope they have improved by now, or we never will have enough teachers!) would have sent me to certain whack-o-woozy land. I was bored to death.

I decided I simply would not make it two more years. But there was that geology class . . .

With all due respect to the science of studying the crust of the earth, sitting day after excruciating day and talking about rocks just about sucked the very life out of my being. I took the class twice and got low grades both times. I could not make my mind apply itself to a study of hard, cold rocks.

I seriously looked at a second option—dropping out of college and going to work. Whoa! That was drastic. An eight-to-five receptionist job? Bad choice for a creative twenty-two year old. I don't remember if we had such things as aptitude tests or guidance counselors, but they wouldn't have done a lot of good anyway. The choices for women were so limited.

As a young person, I felt my world boxing me into a small space. I can remember the very day that I paced back and forth in my room thinking, *There must be another way, a third option out there somewhere. Explore! Think a new thought. Move past your basic assumptions.*

I remembered hearing about a tiny department hidden over in the school of home economics, called applied arts. I had never had any art classes, so I doubted they would even talk to me. But in my desperate state, I dropped by the office.

The short version of the story is that I changed my major to applied arts, and a whole new world opened to me! I loved it, and they didn't mind my lack of previous experience. For the first time in my life, I met other people like me. They didn't like studying rocks either. We thought great design thoughts, enjoyed beautiful things, and created art out of raw materials. After I graduated, I even stayed on and taught some of the basic intro classes. Thank goodness I looked past my first two options.

I have used this method of refusing to accept the given options many, many times since. Sometimes circumstances do limit choices, but rare is the case when you can't find an exciting alternative.

Options should set you free to live with the fewest obstacles. Look for a different light. Look for new possibilities. Look past the destructive, limiting assumptions that have kept you from moving forward. Remember that the words *should have* and *could have* are limiting. Of course, there are no guarantees. Those third and fourth options are often risky situations. But they also often offer the greatest possibilities.

Think of your future as something *you* have control over. *You* can design it. And sometimes a crisis is the perfect time to carefully evaluate the options, refuse to accept the first set of options, and move into a new light. Leave off the old anchors and move into a new potential. Make your dreams a reality.

*Then the LORD said to me, "You have made your way around this hill country long enough; now turn north."*

Deuteronomy 2:2–3

(I use this verse here because it reminds me that I often find myself going in circles, around and around the same nonproductive situations. There comes a time when you must refuse the circles and "turn north" into more fruitful territory.)

# THE WAX AND WANE OF
# THE LIFE WAVE

*A major reason for my depression I'm convinced
was due to my twisted view of God—that He
was a remote, mysterious deity and that I had to
work constantly to try to gain His approval.*

—NANCI CARMICHAEL

The biggest part of my day is over, thank goodness, because I have just had it! I can't give one more ounce of energy to anything! That's too bad, because there are still items on my list that have to be done tonight. But how? I'm exhausted. I don't know what happened to my energy.

I didn't work all that hard today. It was steady, but not a big grizzly day like it could have been. So what's with the tiredness? Actually, the more I think about it, I feel more *blah* than tired, kind of down and depressed like the wane of my wave, like I was being pulled under. Maybe it was the news about that really good program that didn't get funded. Yes, that's when it started. I had worked so hard on that, and now nothing! Just rotten luck. "We regret to inform you, blah, blah, blah."

Aside from that, I didn't have time to get in even a ten-minute walk, much less a thirty-minute walk. Then I went out to lunch and melted into a puddle in the stifling summer heat. This afternoon I realized that yet another numerical report is being required by a funding source. Hey! If I'd wanted to be a statistician, I'd have gone to work for a football team.

When I got home the air conditioning just wasn't keeping up with the heat. And I only needed a few minutes to come up with at least six other bad things about today.

Have you ever noticed when your wave begins to wane and crash, you just sink into the diminishing energy flow? In fact, while I'm drowning here, I might even pick up a few trashy things about yesterday, and maybe even last week.

Maybe I've overstated here a bit, but you get the idea. Once that wave comes crashing in on you, it's like the momentum picks up all the trash from the full length of the beach and dumps it right on your head. Misery seems to attract more misery, and in no time at all, you can find yourself in really bad shape.

Believe it or not, that's normal. Discouragement happens. It's just a temporary downtime. Waves wax and wane; they come and go. These days happen. They catch you off-guard, and you're sucked under the current before you realize what happened. But tomorrow, or at most the day after, the wave will crest again, and you'll be on top of things.

Until then, what can you do during the crash part of a life wave? My advice is to hunker down and wait till it passes over. I have tried everything I can think of during these downtimes. But honestly, I have never been able to talk myself back up, or eat myself back up, or pull myself back up—not until my body and mind were ready.

Listen to what your body and mind are telling you. They are saying that you need some TLC, and you need it now. Chances are you have given and given and given, and you have no more emotional fuel left. If you try to pull up out of the glum before you have given yourself some nurture, you're only going to make the situation worse.

Hunker down and start doing good things for yourself. Fix a nourishing, cool juice drink or a cup of hot tea. I like to add a lemon/lime soft drink to some kind of fruit juice like cranberry juice. It has a little fizz, a little sugar lift, and some antioxidants. It feels and tastes refreshing.

Light good-smelling candles placed all around your bedroom and bath—lots of good candles. Put on your very favorite music. Then take a long, soaking bath or soothing shower. Use the best-smelling soap you can find. Lather and lather, like you are washing the bad mood off your skin. Wrap yourself in a big snugly towel and think, *hug*. Find a comfy, cozy spot in a big chair and sit. Indulge yourself with what you like to do best—read, do needlework, watch TV. Something that requires nothing from you in terms of energy or feedback.

Check your sleep habits. Sometimes my stress levels are higher than I realize, and my sleep becomes restless and dream-driven for a night or two. This causes an underlying fatigue that can lead to dreadful mood swings.

Bend into the dark mood for an evening. Give yourself all the nurture and care you can manage. Don't be afraid to ask others for what you need during this little crash time. When your soul begins to feel rested and loved, it will spring back, and your life wave will crest again.

(Just a note. If these wane days come up often or last for long periods of time, you may be experiencing a case of full-blown depression—a chemical imbalance in the brain that causes long-term downtime. Your doctor can offer you help for it. Run, don't walk, to the nearest medical office and discuss your symptoms.)

*I will exalt you, O LORD, for you lifted me out of the depths and did not let my enemies gloat over me. O LORD my God, I called to you for help and you healed me. O LORD, you brought me up from the grave, you spared me from going down into the pit.*

*You turned my wailing into dancing; you removed my sackcloth and clothed me with joy, that my heart may sing to you and not be silent. O LORD my God, I will give you thanks forever.*

Psalm 30: 1–3, 11–12

*Habitual anger sows suspicion and fear where there should be trust; violence where there should be safety; and hostility where there should be intimacy.* —LISA BEVERE

Clara and I are both Texas women; we enjoy laughing about our strong wills and hard-driving personalities. She is so intelligent and interesting to be around, always smartly dressed and elegant, a real asset to a group in which we are both members. So I was a little surprised when Clara approached me one day and said, "Could you recommend a book on forgiveness? I really need some help." Her face was grim and deadly serious. I could see she was intensely troubled, but obviously didn't want to reveal more details.

Sadly, I had to admit I really was not aware of books on forgiveness, but I assured her I would look around.

I was concerned about Clara, but I am respectful of the privacy of people's battles. When people are ready, the story will come out. Until then I feel I need to offer space and support, so I waited to see if Clara wanted to say more. She didn't.

As plans for this book materialized, I put the word out that I wanted to include stories from other women who had experienced loss in their lives. Within a few weeks I got a call from Clara. "I want to tell my story," Clara said. "I want people to know what I'm going through." So here is her story, in her own words:

A little more than a year ago, my husband had a six-month affair with a woman in another city. At the time, he was commuting weekly there to work. When I discovered the affair, I was stunned, devastated, and almost numb with disbelief. It didn't take long for me to get angry, though. And boy, did I get angry!

As the days and weeks went by, my anger grew, and it wasn't long before I was so full of fury and rage that my family became concerned. I had become obsessed with the anger I felt toward my husband. I felt helpless and hopeless, too. Where could I turn?

When you lose a loved one to death, friends and family and the church rally around to help you get through the difficult time. But when the subject is the death of a marriage and a deeply emotional relationship as well, it is hard to know just where to turn. We just don't talk about these things.

For some reason we are ashamed to ask for solace from friends who love us. I finally got up the nerve to ask my primary care physician for a referral to "see someone" about my emotional difficulty. He referred me to a psychologist, but unfortunately, she did little to help and even made my frustration worse. She wanted to call in my family for group talks, when all I wanted to do was beat the daylights out of my cheating husband. I'm a Texas girl, and our feelings are pure and honest!

Through a referral from one of my son's friends, I did finally find a marriage counselor, which was what we needed. He worked with my husband, who was anxious to save our marriage, and he worked with me. Sometimes we went together, sometimes we each went alone. But the best thing that came from this counseling was that it validated my feelings of anger, which was a wonderful gift to me. Finally, someone said it was OK for me to be so mad! He helped, mostly by pointing us in the right direction and giving us a little shove, but all the work had to be done by us.

Our marriage is mending, but we will never be the same. Time doesn't heal the pain, but it does help you gain perspective. I have prayed, asking for answers. At one point I even got angry with God for not fixing this. I read and researched, trying to find answers and ways to deal with my pain. This tough lady won't give up.

I tell you Clara's story because as I write this book, I can see that she is still dealing with strong feelings of betrayal and a breach of trust. There are no easy answers, and people who offer easy answers are not the ones who have been through the fire.

Issues of forgiveness continuously resound in the lives of many people. Unresolved, these struggles can turn inward where they can wreak havoc, eventually turning into deep depression. Forgiveness is like an ointment that helps heal our inner pain. It releases us to love again. But it is hard, and it takes a lot of work. I have no doubt that with her keen mind and burning desire to overcome, Clara will find the peace she is seeking.

"Fear not, for I have redeemed you; I have summoned you by name; you are mine. When you pass through the waters, I will be with you; and when you pass through the rivers, they will not sweep over you. When you walk through the fire, you will not be burned; the flames will not set you ablaze."

Isaiah 43:1b–2

---

*It was like stepping into a negative rather than a photograph. I was overcome by the sudden realization of the scale of the loss.* —IRENA KLEPFISZ

There it is again! Just when I least expect it, the storm clouds gather and are raining tears down my cheeks before I even realize what has happened.

It has been many months now since I became a single woman. You have already read about my ups and downs and the positive spin I've put on being alone. And it is all true. God has led me gently through thick and thin and given me strength when there was none. He has given me a song in the night and a hymn of gratitude by day.

But every once in awhile, there it is again—sadness, oh such sadness! Oh, what might have been!

I've heard it before, and I know it is true: when you lose a section of your body (arm, toe, foot, leg, breast), it takes awhile for the brain to realize the missing part is actually gone. You think you can still feel it being there. They call this a "phantom foot" (arm, breast, and so on). There are stories of folks recently out of surgery who are going nuts trying to scratch a toe that is no longer there. It is a very strange phenomenon.

I guess that is what this sadness is. Being married for thirty-five years actually requires surgery to separate the partners from one another. We have shared so much, so many good times, so many very difficult times. Sometimes, it was hard to remember where one of us stopped and the other began. Partners. And in some ways, we will always be.

---

That's why the sadness keeps returning every now and then. My brain just hasn't processed the information that a part of me is missing—the phantom partner.

> *The LORD is close to the brokenhearted and saves those who are crushed in spirit.*
>
> Psalm 34:18

# JOURNALING

Keeping a journal is different for different folks. Everyone has their own approach, and they are as varied as humanity itself. My sister, who was living through the ravages of advanced breast cancer, made neat entries each day in her journal book. Her writings brightened with glimpses of hope when she occasionally got a tentative report of remission. Other days testified to her great faith and trust in a loving God. And yes, the sorrow and pain of preparing to leave her family was there as well. The writings were valuable to her family as they read the pages and were able to see how each of them had been in her thoughts.

So many of my experiences are ones where I *feel* but cannot verbalize my feelings. Journaling translates these feelings into words and makes them so much easier to cope with. As I select specific words to describe an impression or a mood or a recess of my heart, I am basically pulling that emotion out of hiding. As I write and think and write some more, I sometimes get to the end of the session and think, "Gee, I had no idea I felt like that!"

Writing in a journal is a way of unpacking my thoughts. Both men and women have been so socialized and cultured that we keep our real feelings hidden away so that we do not offend others or embarrass ourselves. Pretty soon, we have so many unexpressed, repressed feelings and thoughts that the wastebasket fills up. We need an outlet. A private, blank page of paper is just the thing to use in pouring out our heart (or gut, depending on the gender).

Journaling is best if it is not used for recrimination or wrath. I think of my journal as my dearest friend in the world, someone who would never hurt me. I can tell my journal any secret without fear of judgment. However, as I go along, I often reread pages to measure progress or changes, but never by way of berating my words of truth. Journal writing makes me feel valued as a real, feeling person.

And here comes the part I like best. I don't worry about spelling, or grammar, or neatness. As the flow of my consciousness comes streaming out, I let it flow, not stopping to correct words. My spelling is so bad that I just consider it a type of code that only I can read. I thank the computer industry every day for rescuing me with spell check. By the end of a whole manuscript, my spell check is smoking. But in my own journal—who cares? I write what comes.

If you have never kept a journal, it may take awhile to get the hang of it. After all you are conditioned never to let your real feelings show—so what is this when, all of a sudden, you're *supposed* to write real feelings down? Start with easy subjects. The following are a few suggested topics to write about.

- Think of the goodness of God and write about two things you think most represent this goodness.
- Write about a special Christmas you remember as a child and why that year stood out in your memory.

- Describe your favorite hiding place as a child.

- List the talents or characteristics you are most proud of in yourself.

- Ponder a hope or a dream you have for your future and record it.

- Write down your favorite color and tell why it is your favorite. Does it remind you of yourself? How?

- Name the person you would most like to have lunch with—living or dead, anywhere in the world? Why?

- Describe your pet peeves. How do they affect your everyday life?

Privacy is a big concern with journals. Hopefully you live in a household where these private writings are considered sacred possessions that are not to be touched or read by anyone else without your permission. However, discussing your journal entries can be a nice conversation with trusted friends or life partners. I have known women who write, write, and write. They fill a journal, but then destroy it. That seems a little extreme to me, but to each her own. Some journals would be fabulous gifts for inheritance.

*Selecting a journal.* I have purchased many blank journals, and I highly recommend buying spiral-bound books that open fully and stay open. My journal time comes to an abrupt halt if I have to struggle with keeping the pages open. Of course, retail stores offer beautiful and expensive bound journals, but sometimes, just a couple of dollars for a spiral notebook at the drugstore will work. But I think if your life is worth living, it is worth putting the story in a pretty book because it just gives a touch of class.

*Writing utensils*. I bet you never thought that *what* you write with would be important. I like to keep a set of colored pens nearby so that I can select a color to fit my mood or subject. But my main consideration is using good writing instruments. An inexpensive pen constantly leaving blobs of ink or running out of ink just slows me down and takes a lot of the fun out of the experience. The ink should flow as freely as my thoughts.

To me, journal writing is as fun as it is therapeutic. We have a journal-writing group that meets at our senior center. They select a topic, and they all write about it. Then they may choose to read what they wrote. These men and women just rave about how much they value the friendships of those members with whom they have shared their journaling.

I keep quotations in my journal. In a week's time, I run across statements or remarks that strike my fancy. I write them down as I find them, then transfer the ideas to my journal later.

My journal looks more like a scrapbook than anything else. I never know when an idea or thought or situation is going to strike. I have things written on the back of sales slips, paper bags, check stubs, napkins, and church bulletins, all sticking in and hanging out of my journal. I have to capture these moments when they happen; otherwise, the rest of the day's activities will erase them.

Journaling is a habit to cultivate—a very happy habit. It makes me feel like I have a new best friend who thinks just like I do.

*Praise be to the God and Father of our Lord Jesus
Christ, the Father of compassion and the God of
all comfort, who comforts us in all our troubles, so
that we can comfort those in any trouble with the
comfort we ourselves have received from God.*

2 Corinthians 1:3–4

*Some of us act as though our habits were issued at birth and, good or bad, are as predetermined as our blood type and about as likely to ever change. Nothing could be further from the truth.*

—Mary Hunt

Time is a wonderful thing and also a force to be reckoned with. We refer to "running out of time," which, when translated, means, "I crammed too much into a short period of time." We talk about days that are too short or long days that have too much time. Actually all days have the exact same twenty-four hours they have had since the earth started spinning. So what makes a day short or long? The activities we use to fill the hours. Time in a day is the same; how you spend it is different.

The very passage of time constantly changes our lives. Physically and mentally we experience happy times looking forward to a tenth birthday, or apprehensive times as we approach a sixtieth birthday. And at some point in our lives, time seems to speed up, and birthdays come in rapid succession.

Nothing stays the same. Time continues to wear us down, diminishing our bodies like water rounding off rocks. The loss of physical prowess is a part of the passage of time on this earth. Granted, you can follow a healthy lifestyle and attempt to slow the process. Certain medications can improve joints, faulty heartbeats, and various other wearing-out parts. But, in truth, sooner or later, most of us will slow to a different pace.

Sooner or later, we will pass a store window or mirror and be shocked to discover what time has done to our appearances. A difficult leave-taking of the beautiful, young, 115-pound woman with peaches-and-cream skin who smiled with perfect teeth and not a wrinkle showing. Where has that beautiful woman gone? What has time done to me?

Frankly, I grieve that loss. I just cannot get accustomed to living with the person I see in the mirror. My mind knows that my core being is still the same—or better. The person I am now is probably wiser, more sensitive to others, and not as fearful as the younger woman was. I realize I can look back over a full, active, and very happy life. And I know, beyond any doubt, that I still have excellent health. I ain't done yet!

But I miss walking into a store and going to size-eight dresses. I miss being able to climb stairs without groaning. I miss being able to follow a two year old around without getting tired. Yes, friends, to be truthful, time has not been kind to my appearance or to my stamina. I simply have to let go of what I used to look like and begin to accept what I have to work with now.

I know I'm not alone in this. More honest, maybe, but not alone. Every article you read on aging discusses the thief called time. So, what do we do?

Get busy, that's all. *To everything there is a season.* Find out what season your life is in and jump into the middle of the action—at whatever pace you can manage! Change your labels and thus your perceptions. How about calling yourself "Wise Woman of Age"? What about "Matriarch"? Doesn't that sound regal?

Move with confidence and grace into the future. As my body changes, time cannot rob me of true beauty, charm, grace, or a proud and majestic carriage. Time can never take away a happy, optimistic, accepting, and expectant attitude. Time can't touch a pleasant disposition.

Indeed, time is giving me an opportunity to experience a broader life. Come to think of it, perhaps it is the *pursuit of youth* that robs, not time.

Good-bye, youth. Hello, richer, fuller life.

*Moon shell, who named you? Some intuitive woman I like to think. I shall give you another name—Island shell. I cannot live forever on my island. But I can take you back to my desk in Connecticut.* —ANNE MORROW LINDBERGH

On my desk is a small glass dish with a collection of delicate seashells. Being a West Texas girl, I didn't grow up knowing about shells and sand and beaches. That was an adult experience for me. And what an experience it was! The first time I encountered a real canonical shell, I thought I would cry. It was one of the most beautiful, perfectly formed pieces of sculpture I had ever seen.

It ranked right up there with my three absolute *top* nature experiences: a tiny hummingbird nest with two eggs, a baby owl on my front porch, and a *double* rainbow that reached from horizon to horizon. Each of these sights absolutely brought me to my knees in total adoration of the Creator. And now, the shells. They were so beautiful! And one was cut so that I could see the little separate chambers built in perfect succession.

Normally I would never capture any of these glorious nature items except on film, but the seashells were different. The ones I saw first were in a shell shop, and the little critters who used the shells for shelter had long since moved on. I felt I was on solid ecological ground to purchase and enjoy them.

I also purchased several books on shells, because I rarely enjoy just looking at anything. When I am truly fascinated, I want to know *all* about them—under what conditions does nature produce such a glorious item? Where? When? How long does it take? So I read and collected shells and became more and more captivated by this true marvel of the Great Creator.

Lucky for you, I won't give my full five-dollar lecture on seashells here, but I do want to mention the most amazing part of all. Did you know that each canonical shell is built in perfect mathematical regularity? Each chamber of that shell is built in exact ascending dimensions to the chamber before. That's what makes the shells strong enough to withstand the great pressures of ocean water. And this logarithmic spiral is the same form found in ram horns and even the path of a moth flying toward light. Can you believe what magnificent miracles we live in and around?

Now scientists tell me that this is no miracle; it is a law of nature and the shells are formed by "struggle for life" evolution. I do not have a problem with that. I call it a miracle; they call it an evolution. I say it *all* goes back to the God of Creation, one way or another.

Just think, the same God who threw the moon and stars into space and set the world in motion also sculpted this tiny habitat. And that same God put me here and made me special in the same way—and now loves me more each day. God loved, God created—He set it all in intricate motion, and we are free to enjoy.

The shells on my desk are a constant source of pleasure for me. When I look at these wonders, how can I ever doubt His mercy and care for me?

*When I consider your heavens, the work of your fingers, the moon and the stars, which you have* set in place, what is man that you are mindful of him, the son of man that you care for him? You made him a little lower than the heavenly beings and crowned him with glory and honor. You made him ruler over the works of your hands; you put everything under his feet: all flocks and herds, and the beasts of the field, the birds of the air, and the fish of the sea, all that swim the paths of the seas. O LORD, our Lord, how majestic is your name in all the earth!

Psalm 8:3–9

*Don't be deceived, my dear brothers. Every good and perfect gift is from above, coming down from the Father of the heavenly lights, who does not change like shifting shadows.* —JAMES 1: 16–17

Many years ago, when my husband and I were married, one of the church members gave us a gift that looked like a set of dueling pistols. Actually it was a sizable carving set, a knife and fork large enough to carve a whole buffalo. The two utensils had pistol-type handles and fit together in a holder that looked as if it could have been mounted on a castle wall. We were speechless when we opened the velvet case. It was so ugly, so out of proportion, and so useless, there simply was no comment that fit the situation. The silence that followed led her to see she had made a big error in selecting that gift. So the giver tried to explain, "Well, I know that is a very strange gift, but then, you all are so . . . " and her voice quickly trailed off as she realized her ship was going down faster than she could bail herself out. At that point there was no redemption for anyone. We just laughed and moved on, then disposed of the carving set as soon as we could.

That experience now stands as my supreme example of bad gift giving. Did she not think? Or was that a gift from her own collection of interesting artifacts?

There is a real art to gift giving, and that nice lady obviously had missed out on the fine points of the art. As I survey the whole gift-giving mechanism, I can see three kinds of gifters: people who *hate* giving gifts, people who give but mostly rely on thoughtless obligation, and folks who *love* giving gifts and really throw themselves into the process to make fun choices. They give often and thoughtfully. Giving and receiving requires a stroke of creativity and finesse, but with a few guidelines even the most ardent non-giver can get in on the fun.

As an old-fashioned gift giver, I am basically appalled at today's practices of the retail-driven gift registry. I know what the benefits are, and I even manage to accept a china-and-silver-pattern registry. But recently, a bride and groom went way beyond the usual registry; they posted a wish list on their Web site. Then they would check off the gifts as they received them. Pleeeease! This is not gift giving; this is shopping.

What happened to friendship and making personal selections based on love and affection? That couple may have received everything on their list, but they got precious few *gifts,* which are tokens of your fondness for other people. The gift should reflect *your* taste and *their* style as you see it. It should be personal enough that every time they use, or look at, the gift, they are reminded of you and your thoughtfulness. Excuse me, but I just don't see how a screwdriver from a home repair store fits that description!

Gifts should never be chosen based on monetary value. A well-thought-out gift does not have to wreck your budget. And giving with a sense of competition with other gifts and givers cancels the whole experience.

I personally think handmade gifts are the best, if you can manage it. These can be tailor-made to suit any person for any occasion. A favorite of mine are small "chat pillows" with funny sayings either stitched or painted on the fabric. "Life ain't always an uptown Saturday night," or "If the broom fits, fly it," or "Well-behaved women seldom make history"—all are real conversation pillows for lucky recipients. Then I finish them with beautiful fabric backing and fringe around the edges. They are time consuming, but inexpensive, and make a big statement about your thoughtfulness.

A second favorite gift of mine is something from an art seller or an antique store. All these choices require search time, but in my thinking, that is part of the gift. One year we had a big Christmas open house and needed music. A dear friend graciously agreed to play the piano for us. In exchange, I was able to find an antique wooden tambourine as a gift. He loved it and kept it on his own piano for years.

The best gifts are spontaneous, with no special occasion in mind. My sister-in-law is a great gift giver. Out of the blue, for no reason at all, gifts arrive just as a wild-hair surprise. And it's never anything I could have found at a store. Just a wonderful, creative surprise that is fun to get and absolutely makes my day. The other day another friend sent me a little package that contained tissues printed with Volkswagen Beetles, a little eraser shaped like a Beetle, and a note pad shaped like a Beetle. She included a note that said, "I know you like Beetles. I thought of you when I saw these."

My specialty is buying for folks "who have *everything,*" and what they don't have, they could go out and buy. What a challenge to think of something that might give them a chuckle or a smile and still won't break my bank account. I plot and plan for days to come up with an idea that just perfectly suits the occasion—a special dinner at my place, or tickets to a small theater performance, or a fancy key tassel, or a small painting by an unknown (and inexpensive) artist. And on the chance that my friends don't *want* it, or don't *like* it, or don't *need* it, no matter! I've had the fun of giving, they knew I put a lot of thought into the gift, and that's what's important.

I never try to "match" gifts: in other words, I do not buy something expensive because I received something expensive. I have friends who could buy and sell me several times over, but this fact cannot, and should not, influence my gift giving. I'm not trying to meet a *need* of theirs—heaven knows they can do that for themselves. I just want to show them I'm thinking about them and value their friendships.

To make gifts special, I always include personalized, hand-written notes to express my appreciation for their friendships or relationships or for other reasons. A well-written note will add even more value to the gift. An old book found at an antique mall or old bookstore becomes a special treasure when accompanied by a note saying why you thought of the person when you purchased the book.

Giving and receiving should always reflect the spirit of the Greatest Gift given—given freely and given in love.

*For God so loved the world that he gave his one and only Son, that whoever believes in him shall not perish but have eternal life.*

John 3:16

# The Hum of That Sewing Machine Is Like Music to My Ears

*Memories are crucial to our existence. Without them, we wouldn't know who we are. Memories give us our own personal history, a history that defines us and gives substance to our being.*

—Bernie Sheahan

The pressure foot lowers over the carefully placed fabric. I search for the foot pedal with my bare foot and start moving the stitches across the fabric. I figure I have sewn about a hundred million trillion miles of stitches on that old sewing machine. It's the first thing I purchased with money I earned at a real job in the big world.

Many times, back in my younger married years, I "took in" sewing for other people to earn extra money. I made clothes, curtains, decorative items, wall hangings, anything. I even made a wedding dress for a friend who couldn't afford a ready-made outfit.

I also make little girl dresses for my two grandbabies—Easter dresses with yellow ducks and red-smocked dresses for Christmas. I made curtains for Abigail's room in her new house just like my mother made for me.

There are fancy new machines that think for you, sew for you, and almost sing and dance for you as they turn out beautiful garments. But for me, I love my old machine—nearly forty years we've been together. We're like old friends; we understand each other.

You see, sewing is like looking at an old photo album. My grandmother, whom I called Mama Dear, taught me to sew when I was barely able to reach my little feet to make the pedal go back and forth. Some of my most treasured possessions are the little doll clothes she and I constructed. She had drawers full of scrap fabric all neatly rolled and pinned into little bundles. I could use any of it I wanted. Then I could search through the bits-and-pieces box and select rick-rack or lace or buttons to go on the doll dresses. We, of course, didn't have Barbie dolls with their little body parts; we sewed for my baby doll, Cookie. And she did look so lovely in her special styled wardrobe. The hours I spent with my patient, loving grandmother were priceless. Every time I sit at my machine I can see that picture clearly.

My mother, too, is an expert seamstress. She was blessed with a sense of excellent style and beautiful understanding of how to put smart looks together. This was somewhat of a problem for a preacher's wife, because there simply wasn't a budget to support a smart style. Undaunted, my mother would head to the nearest fabric store and start her perusal through the *Vogue* pattern books. After some heavy-duty decision making, pairing fabric and pattern, my mother would confidently head for home and the sewing machine. She approached those projects with all the intensity of Joshua conquering Jericho.

I can remember the scene well—fragile tissue pattern sheets spread out expertly on that fabric. Scissors, tapes, a chalkwheel, and mother with a mouth full of pins. She would labor and sew, and fret and rip out what she had sewn and start again because she wanted it done exactly right.

We have laughed/cried (a combination of the two emotions) many times as the newly finished garment failed to meet her standards and went straight to Goodwill without ever being worn.

The hum of those three sewing machines link our generations together like strong chains. If we developed a female coat of arms for our family, a needle and thread would be right in the middle.

And you can bet your life that those old doll dresses will be pulled out in the years to come with stories to my granddaughters about their great-great-grandmother and their great-grandmother and the importance of the sewing machine.

I wish I still had Mama Dear's old pedal machine, but it was lost in the shuffle of moves and life changes. I do have one exactly like it, though, that I keep in my bedroom beside the big wicker rocker. Her picture sits on a nearby table. I know it's not true, but I sure feel like I can hear the hum of that faraway machine, when I sit and listen. "Here's how you do it, Susie. Put your gathering thread across the top of the little sleeve."

*Dear Lord, how thankful I am for my heritage, for my memories, and for the women who taught me the skills of sewing. Thank You for the good times, and the very important life lessons I learned with a needle and thread in hand.*

*Day by day, we make a daily choice to meet with Him about the day He has gifted us with.* —Jill Briscoe

While Jesus was on earth, His disciples must have observed Him talking to God many times. We have records of a few of those observations.

*After he had dismissed them, he went up on a mountainside by himself to pray. When evening came, he was there alone.*

Matthew 14:23

*Then Jesus went with his disciples to a place called Gethsemane, and he said to them, "Sit here while I go over there and pray."*

Matthew 26:36

As His followers went through their daily travels of preaching, teaching, and ministry, there must have been times when they wondered where Jesus got His compassion, His passion, and His endurance to withstand the continual draw on His strength. I can imagine, based on the information we have, that Jesus would stop the trip, maybe go off a short distance into a close meadow, sit on a low stone wall, and talk to God, the disciples observing.

No doubt the followers, even in their lack of total understanding, did grasp the concept that these conversations with God were a source of great strength and power for their Teacher.

Can't you see them sitting there with puzzled looks on their faces, then voicing their ideas: "You know, we need to learn how to do that. Praying is an important part of who Jesus is. Maybe, if we knew what it was all about. . . ." And so they asked, "Lord, teach us."

I think one of the more interesting points of this request is that the disciples realized that prayer was a *learned* art, not just a quick list of "help me's" and "give me's." They did not confuse wishes, hopes, laments, or even rejoicings with prayer. Prayer is so much more than pouring out one's needs to God.

In order to pray, we need the Holy Spirit, and we pray through Jesus Christ. Or in the case of the disciples, they needed Jesus to help them pray. It is a painful experience to stand before the throne of God, speechless, with every call to Him falling back at our feet. In this need we search for the Holy Spirit through Jesus to lead us to prayer.

I think this is a basis for prayer partners. Going hand-in-hand with a prayer partner into the presence of God can be a very powerful thing. We learn from each other and we draw strength to pray from one another.

Jesus often prayed using the words God had already given in the Old Testament. Today, if we wish to pray with confidence, then looking to words of prayer already given in the Bible is a solid place to start.

*Praise the LORD, O my soul;*
*    all my inmost being, praise his holy name.*
*Praise the LORD, O my soul,*
*    and forget not all his benefits—*
*who forgives all your sins*
*    and heals all your diseases,*

who redeems your life from the pit
and crowns you with love and compassion,
who satisfies your desires with good things
so that your youth is renewed like the eagle's.
                                                    Psalm 103:1–5

The book of Psalms is an entire book of prayers written by King David and various other writers. Some were set to music and used in worship services; others seem to have been spoken by David himself in times of great travail. But all are recorded in the power of the Spirit of God. Considering this, we recognize the extraordinary way in which God teaches us to pray. Begin to "pray through" the book of Psalms. Let God's prayers be your prayers.

Hear my prayer, O LORD;
let my cry for help come to you.
Do not hide your face from me
when I am in distress.
Turn your ear to me;
when I call, answer me quickly.
                                                    Psalm 102:1–2

*Lord, open the doors I need to walk through today. Close the doors I don't.* —THELMA WELLS

Sara was at the airport to watch fifteen of her church friends leave on a nineteen-day mission trip to Africa. For weeks, she had helped them plan, assemble, and pack dozens of crates with materials, supplies, tools, and literature. She had been a part of the initial stages when they had prayed, accepted the challenge, and then moved to action. The young adults would lead services, help build a church, set up a library, and work with the children—all of which Sara would have loved to have been a part.

The friends all boarded the plane for their long journey to the Gambia. Sara watched them leave. She is very gregarious, a very dedicated Christian, and a firm believer in missions. Her money, her ideas, and her prayers had all gone wholeheartedly and lovingly into this mission trip. She would have been a big asset to the trip. Her organizational skills and bright enthusiasm would have been a help when the going bogged down.

But it was not to be. Sara's fragility just wouldn't mix with the limited living conditions of the destination. Her cognitive self knew this, but her spirit wanted so badly to climb on that plane and be a part of this Good News trip. Instead, it would be Sara's job to pray and encourage from this side of the world.

The group set up a Web site and posted daily notes, messages, reports, and photos of their work. Sara was able to keep up with everyone on a daily basis;

she in turn was able to support the mission with fervent prayers and encouraging messages.

Weeks later, when they returned, Sara was at the airport waiting with hugs and welcomes for everyone. When our church minister, who was a member of the team, deplaned, he said, "Sara you were so much a part of this trip, I fully expected to look up and see you coming in the door every morning. Your prayer notes and encouragement kept us going."

*There are different kinds of gifts, but the same Spirit. There are different kinds of service, but the same Lord. There are different kinds of working, but the same God works all of them in all men.*
                                    I Corinthians 12:4–6

*Life is made up of desires that seem big and vital one minute, and little and absurd the next. I guess we get what's best for us in the end.*

—ALICE CALDWELL RICE (1870–1942)

If torture were to come back in style, any enemy of mine would have an easy task. For me, absolute total and complete torture would be to give me sticky fingers (yuck!) and put me in a long checkout line. Actually you wouldn't need both of these torments; I could be driven near crazy with one or the other.

A woeful lack of patience is a major flaw in my creation. I don't know if God just forgot to give me any, or if this is my thorn in the flesh, so to speak. Or if it is His way of continually testing me. Whatever the reason, two minutes of waiting is just about my limit—whether it's in a checkout line or a string of traffic, or at a restaurant, a red light, or at the doctor's office.

My oldest son, taking after his father, can wait in any line indefinitely. Show him a line, and he will stand in that line until someone comes to tell him to stop standing there. I don't know how he does that. He has patience—all he needs or can ever use. What a blessing!

Someone obviously penned a volume of psychology on the art of waiting. If you have ever been to one of the Disney theme parks, you notice how the lines are wrapped around this way and that, so no one is really aware of how long those lines really are. Then wisely, they put little signs along the way, giving more hope as to how much longer the wait will be. Whether the time is accurate or not, just the hope of only ten more minutes calms your nerves.

Some things make waiting seem even longer: perceived unfairness (the line next to you is clipping right along), anxiety (waiting at the hospital), or unexplained waiting (is there a wreck up ahead?).

With this in mind, I read in the Bible that I'm suppose to be still and *wait* on the Lord.

> *Wait for the LORD; be strong and take heart and wait for the LORD.*
>
> Psalm 27:14

> *Yet the LORD longs to be gracious to you; he rises to show you compassion. For the LORD is a God of justice. Blessed are all who wait for him!*
>
> Isaiah 30:18

Wait! How can I do that? With action whirling all around me, a dozen things to do, deadlines breathing down my neck, I don't have time to *wait*. I must move forward with haste!

But I know better. Moving ahead beyond God's leadership is just time wasted. The writing will not be inspired, the deadlines won't be met with quality pages. It just doesn't work. And what do I miss by rushing ahead and being unable to wait? Peace, understanding, a better quality of life. I'm always so anxious to get finished or get to my destination first, I completely miss the journey.

Wouldn't it be nice, if the next time I'm caught in a standing line, I could spend the time being pleasant to folks around me? When waiting in traffic, I could use the time to pray, praising God for the opportunity to be driving on open, safe streets.

*Dear Lord, help my body and my mind to be more attuned to a patient lifestyle. Help me use my wait time to further the kingdom instead of rushing through to the next event. Help me be more responsive to the journey and less focused on the destination.*

# ENERGY BOOST

## THOUGHTS ON SELF-ESTEEM

*The integrity and self-esteem gained from winning the battle against extremity are the richest treasures in my life.* —DIANA NYAD, CHAMPION MARATHON SWIMMER

*I*n years past, low self-esteem has nudged its way into my life. I offer the following suggestions for defeating it certainly not as an expert, but as one who has been down this path before. One of the values of having lived for a number of years is that I can look at self-esteem with hindsight and foresight—and sometimes even side-sight as I see how self-esteem works or doesn't work in other women.

This is what I have experienced about learning to like and value yourself as a person of worth.

1. Many, many women from all walks of life struggle with self-worth issues. At one time this was a surprise to me. I thought just the opposite—that I was the only one. Even recently when Kathryn Graham, publisher of the *Washington Post*, died, almost every one of her friends and acquaintances described her

self-doubts, her constant feelings of being unprepared for her roles in life. From where I'm sitting, she had it all—looks, charm, intelligence, money, prestige, opportunity, position. What could possibly give her pause for self-doubt? The only conclusion to draw is that self-esteem comes from a source deep inside yourself. It cannot be defined with external trappings. Doubts cannot be resolved by getting richer or thinner or throwing material possessions at them.

2. The term *self-esteem* has been used so much that we now have too many preconceived ideas about it. Many of us have already dismissed or rationalized our position on self-esteem. That leaves us with way too much garbage to sift through before we can get at the real issues. So, let's start using the term *self-appreciation* because it seems to me that is the core element—how much you appreciate yourself as a contributing member of a society/family/job/friendship group. That's what we want to consider—what can we do to rid ourselves of outside evaluation and focus on appreciating ourselves.

3. It has been suggested to me—in books, lectures, talks, and even in therapy—that low self-appreciation has its roots in earliest childhood. From birth, our caregivers teach us whether we are valuable or not. Well, okay, I'll buy that. Thank goodness someone figured that out so we can do a better job with our little tykes now, teaching them to value others and themselves.

With this thought in mind, it is not difficult to look at our pasts and pinpoint specific examples of where our self-understanding was clearly defined in a negative way by some well-meaning adult.

One of those times for me was in the first grade. I was a very shy, scared little girl who was not sure about being in a classroom. I learned immediately that teacher-pleasers received all kinds of quick and positive rewards. So I worked hard to please. One day the teacher returned the homework papers she had just graded. (Today, *graded* papers in first grade raise red flags.) Across the top of my paper, in big letters and red ink, she wrote "EXCELLENT." It was written in cursive, which, of course, I couldn't read, and the "X" in the word was prominent. It stood out like a light. *I had received an "X" on my paper!* Then to make this complete humiliation public, she called me to the front of the room and asked me to hold my paper up for all to see. She said I was an *"Xelent"* student.

Needless to say, my school days were heavily influenced by that drastic misunderstanding, and for many years that memory defined my self-worth, as I saw it.

You probably have a story like that. A moment when you can remember coming to the conclusion that you were not as good, not as smart, not as worthy, not as cute as your peers. It happens.

But, you know what? That's over now! I have since learned what *excellent* means. I know how to spell it. I know that "X" is just one of the letters in the word. That event and others like it from my childhood are over, past, finished. I can move on—*if I want to.* Or I can continue to feel bad about getting an "X" on my paper. It is up to me!

Many times, we carry that heavy childhood baggage for so *long,* dragging it along into every relationship, every situation. We thought we were stuck with it. Those memories are hard to carry, they are debilitating, and certainly they can continue to influence our self-appreciation. What a huge relief it is to set that baggage down! We're not stuck with it. The event is over. Move on.

If we hold on to past experiences, we can use them as tactics for staying in a self-destructive pattern. As long as we can blame our parents, our heavy doses of religion, our teachers, our spouses, our races, or whatever, it is unlikely we will be able to move very far beyond them. Blame is a nice little tuffet to sit upon for really good pity parties, but it is not much help for a growing self-appreciation program.

4. How much do you let other people and events beyond your control define and evaluate you? The answer to this will determine your level of self-appreciation. Life events—rejection, separation, job loss, big whammies!—can bog you down. Your boss can evaluate your work performance. Your spouse can suggest how he wants your relationship to proceed. Friends can describe how to improve your times together. But if these people have your best interests at

heart, then they will use these evaluation times as a give-and-take experience where you *both* define the problems and modifications.

Don't we wish it always worked that way? Instead, we sometimes have negative experiences that beat us over the head emotionally. Then we are crushed by a volley of destructive thoughts. And we believe them! If our bosses said so, it must be right! Oh yeah? And if our husbands said our skills are woefully lacking as housekeepers, we immediately believe that to be true and think it defines our worth. Oh yeah?

Don't let other people define who you are! You don't have to believe what they say. Other people can be *wrong*, you know. No one's character can be defined by a layer of dust under the bed.

We can begin to *give ourselves* what we wish we had received from other people—appreciation. It's true, in my case, that you can write a word in the dust that has collected under my writing table. It's awful. But does that define me? No. There are a lot of accomplishments of which I am proud.

The more consistent and convincing our own self-appreciation is, the less we will have to rely on receiving it from others.

5. Start a card file of appreciative comments. I'm serious about this. Talking, reading, and thinking are good, but seeing your positive attributes in writing packs a much larger wallop. Write statements about why you are a grand, super person. You can write about your accomplishments, looks, job-related successes, parenting

skills—anything at all. Add to the file as you think of things.

Because I am a highly visual person, I use brightly colored cards with colored ink *and stickers!* Fun little stickers of flowers or borders or suns or smiley faces. It makes the statement even *more* important, don't you see?

I go through my card file on a periodic basis so I can visualize what those cards look like. This is my self-appreciation file. My positive self talk. When I am tempted to bow under the pressure of an another person trying to define my character, I remember my file! I don't have to accept their looks of disapproval, or their tone of voice, or the rolling of their eyes, or their words. I *know* better.

6. Remind yourself that you are a person of worth! God thinks so; He created you that way. I can tell you that. Your spouse and your children can tell you that. Your Mama can tell you that. (And don't we love it when they do.) But the truth is, until you tell *yourself* that, nothing else really matters. This is a gift you must give yourself. You are wonderful because *you* say so. Be pleased with yourself. Focus on all you love and like about yourself.

7. Do things you are proud of. I can't speak for other people, but in my own life, I have to continue to do things I feel good about. Taking a risk and succeeding is just about the best feeling there is. It feeds your self-appreciation like nothing else can. Change a relationship that isn't working, change jobs, take a trip, meet someone new—whatever offers a

big, big challenge. Then work *hard* to make the venture a success. It will be a self-appreciation rush you won't soon forget. (And don't forget to write it on a card for the appreciation file.)

8. And my favorite self-appreciation tip of all: *Act* as though you are something special—especially if you're feeling a little underappreciated. You remember the song in *The King and I?* The one that suggests you whistle a happy tune when you feel afraid? It works! When you fool the folks around you, you fool yourself as well. Lift your chin, hold your shoulders back, lift your eyebrows, smile, put some pep in your step, even a little swagger. And whistle or hum. It is a big boost to your self-appreciation! It is hard to be very down on yourself in that posture.

Remember that God loves you. He made you special, a one-of-a-kind person, with talents, ideas, and everything it takes to have a good life. And that is no small consideration. The great, good God of the entire universe is on your side with gifts you have not even begun to use.

*In all these things we are more than conquerors through him who loved us. For I am convinced that neither death nor life, neither angels nor demons, neither the present nor the future, nor any powers, neither height nor depth, nor anything else in all creation, will be able to separate us from the love of God that is in Christ Jesus our Lord.*

Romans 8:37–39

*If thou givest a benefit, keep it close; but if thou receivest one, publish it, for that invites another.*

—ELIZABETH GRYMESTON (1563–1603)

One of the more curious aspects of Jesus' teachings is the absence of His specifically mentioning the tithe as a standard of giving. As important a teaching as that was in the Old Testament, Jesus seems, at first glance, to have rather skimmed over the need to bring 10 percent of one's possessions into "the storehouse."

Old Testament worship was most specific on making sacrifices and gifts, whether it would be the first fruits or the best, unblemished livestock. Even the very poor could purchase a lowly pigeon to bring to the temple for sacrifice. The law was simple and straightforward.

Actually it would have been much easier if Jesus had followed the Old Testament laws with illustrations and parables on giving 10 percent of one's income to the church. That is such a nice, neat, measurable goal. Even a fourth grader can figure 10 percent of his allowance, plop it into the collection plate, and move into a state of righteousness.

Even without Jesus' specific 10 percent allocation, we still fall into debate. Christian people frequently turn into full-blown Pharisees and have to seriously discuss if the 10 percent tithe should be figured on one's *net* or *gross* income!

My friend, if you have ever asked that question, or entertained the thought of that question, you have completely missed the point of all New Testament teaching. And, in my small, human way, I wonder if that is not the exact reason Jesus never got specific on *amounts* of tithes or gifts. He might have known we would go the way of splitting hairs and dividing pennies. Heaven forbid that we contribute one farthing more than required.

The way of a Christ-centered life is *giving!* Period! A tithe is only the beginning. And it doesn't matter if you figure on a gross or net number, because as a Christian, you're going to go so far past a tithe, it won't matter anyway.

This is a difficult and devastating principle for present-day America. Our orientation is on building portfolios, trying to beat the stock market at its own seesaw game. We have large homes to furnish, children to raise and educate. Times are uncertain. Jobs are uncertain. Social security is uncertain. Coming out of the financial boom of the eighties and nineties has left us feeling we must hoard and grasp for treasure to sustain us through our years on this earth. We think of life in terms of accrual and depletion, not share and give.

And even if the stock market somehow leaves us with a coffer brimful, we immediately go into *guard* mode and try to protect our gains as best we can.

My grandmother sometimes went without food for herself, even though there was more than enough money in the bank to provide for her to eat well for the rest of her life. But her guard-and-hoard mentality left her living on a shoestring.

What is it, when we get so locked into accumulating (buy, buy, buy), hoarding, and guarding that it clouds our vision of what is expected of us?

Jesus taught that only in giving do we actually accumulate treasure: *If anyone would come after me, she must deny herself and take up her cross and follow me. For whoever wants to save her life will lose it, but whoever loses her life for me and for the gospel will save it (paraphrased from Mark 8:34b–35).*

Jesus taught that by going well beyond the tithe and becoming so immersed in loving others and caring for others, we are in a state of constant giving—money, time, and especially self. Instead of diminishing our holdings, this form of giving *replenishes* our lives.

Giving with a sincere heart is essential to a complete life. It is what keeps us sane. It keeps us centered in Christ. Giving produces joy and contentment. Giving connects us to God and opens our hearts to know Him better.

Accumulating, buying, and hoarding does none of this. Instead, it draws you in on yourself, makes your life smaller, tighter, and more lonely.

Give! Reach out to others. Notice service people who wait on you. Tip generously. Treat people with respect. Look for need in your immediate surroundings. Give and enjoy life. To live is to give.

*Dear Lord, in a world woefully in need of Your love and Your saving grace, may I always answer the need in whatever way I can—sometimes with goods, sometimes with care and attention, and sometimes leading folks to a safe harbor. Help me to see need as You saw need and help me, most of all, to respond to need as You responded.*

---

*And I said to the man who stood at the gate of the year: "Give me a light that I may tread safely into the Unknown." And he replied: "Go out into the darkness and put your hand into the hand of God. That shall be to you better than light, and safer than a known way."*

—MINNIE HASKINS (1875–1957)

About once a year, our newspaper runs a long list of names, sometimes taking up several pages, of folks who have money, real estate, or inheritance coming to them, but for some reason the assets have not been claimed. Can you imagine having a rich aunt that you didn't even know existed? That in itself would be a big surprise. But on top of that, what if she died and left you $10,000 and you didn't even know it? That money has been sitting in a lawyer's office somewhere for years just waiting for you to claim it.

Yeah, right! Being the skeptic I am, that is a little hard to believe! But don't tell anyone I search that list with all the expectation of a winner. Just think if that were true and I found myself $10,000 richer than I ever expected! Hidden, surprise money!

Well, I can't promise you a way to find surprise money, but I can give you a hint that is almost as good. You do have many assets you have forgotten about, or are not using. I guarantee it.

Years ago, when the children were young, we decided to make out our wills so we could leave specific arrangements for the children in case of our early and unexpected departures. The lawyer took down all the information and discussed the various options for handling our financial assets. He inquired as to the estimate of our estate. We both about died on the spot from laughing. What estate? What assets?

The lawyer, who was a good friend, didn't laugh. He assured us there was an estate and that we would be surprised at what value was there, if we started listing. He suggested we go home and make a list of all the things we owned, including insurance policies. We did and we *were* surprised! We weren't rich folks by any means, but when it was all added together on paper, we were better off than we thought. With better management and an understanding of our assets, we could begin to build a nice nest egg.

When I think about it, I'm reasonably sure this same plan could work with personal assets, also. You are probably walking around with enough talent, experience, connections, and knowledge to do just about anything you would ever want to do. Did you read that correctly? You are probably in command of any number of talents and abilities that have been dormant for so long, you don't even know you have them.

I'm reminded of one of my dad's favorite Bible stories—the conversation between Moses and God concerning what assets Moses had that he was completely unaware of (Exodus 4). God had a big job waiting for Moses; He needed a leader for the children of Israel, someone to get them out of Egypt. But Moses begged God to let someone else do it. Moses pleaded that he was not eloquent enough; he was "slow in speech and tongue." In other words, he was too shy, he had no qualifications to be a leader of any kind, much less the kind of leader God was looking for.

But God, in essence, instructed Moses that with divine help, he had *everything* he needed to work with. In a question, God said, "What is that in your hand?" Moses replied that all he had was a staff. Then God showed Moses that if a staff was what he had, God could use that for good.

To this day I can hear my daddy standing behind the pulpit, with his hand outstretched, using his big, booming preacher voice to ask, "What do you have in your hand? Use it for God!" Many a soul responded to that question under my dad's preaching.

And now I ask you the same. Look at your personal assets. Then look again at what they might be under God's blessing. You have anything and everything you need to be what God wants you to be. If those assets are hidden, as if still in your rich aunt's account, pull them out, develop them, then offer what you have to God. You have the assets to achieve what you need to do.

> *In your unfailing love you will lead*
> *the people you have redeemed.*
> *In your strength you will guide them*
> *to your holy dwelling.*
>
> Exodus 15:13

*Learning to turn loose of what we cannot change is not only one of life's most difficult lessons but one of its most important.* —RICHARD EXLEY

*T*his would be our first Christmas after we had all moved into our separate dwellings. I hardly knew how to plan or what to do. I had gone from decorating a big nine-room house to now decorating three rooms. I spent anguished hours sorting through our Christmas treasures to decide what very few could be used. It was an emotional time as I looked at each decoration and remembered the time, the place, and the circumstance in which we added that piece to our collection. I sobbed as I had to pack item after item back in the box, unable to find a place for most of it.

I made selections based on the earliest items, which would remind us of long ago Christmases when the children were young.

It was like putting a treasured yet broken glass bowl back together. Somehow I had to take the broken pieces of our family—with all the pain and hurt and miscommunications—and glue them back together to make a real Christmas. How on earth could it be done?

I called each of the children and gently interviewed them. How do you want us to do Christmas this year? Where do you want to have Christmas dinner? Hesitantly they all agreed, "Let's do it like we always do. We want everyone together, like it used to be. And we want to be at your place."

Frankly, I think if we had all been truthful, we would have all taken a rain check on the holidays that year. But probably, for my sake, and for lack of a better plan, they all voted to proceed with a "regular" family Christmas. So I continued with the decorating, the cooking, and the planning. I would do my best to construct a happy family holiday with all our broken pieces.

The good news was that we had a precious little Christmas angel to help us celebrate for the first time—Abigail was nine months old and as cute as a baby could be. While this was certainly a happy attraction, it also might highlight my lack of space and our crowded conditions.

Mother also was coming from Texas to be with us. Having all the generations together adds a particular goodness to Christmas.

Then, one night, about ten days before the Christmas day, I was sitting quietly, making final lists of last minute gifts and groceries. The phone rang and Sara's friend said, "You'd better come; Sara is hurt!" I got directions and went stone cold. That could only mean one thing—a broken leg, an emergency room, surgery, a big body cast, and pain and suffering beyond endurance. *Oh, dear God, please don't let this happen now. Please let this not be true! Not this year, please God!*

As I drove to the restaurant where they were, I tried to stay as calm as possible. We carefully got Sara into the van and headed to the hospital. So much for Christmas. When Sara is hurt, our lives pretty much grind to a dead stop while we try to care for her and try to soothe our own troubled souls. In all these years, we have not been able to get a grip on watching her suffer. It tears us to pieces every time.

A few days later, she and I got home from the hospital—cast and all. At this point Sara and cast weighed a little over one hundred pounds. So not only did we participate in the suffering, but we had to creatively devise all kinds of caretaking strategies. It was a 24/7 situation. We transformed my three rooms into a guest room for Mother, a hospital room for Sara, and a Christmas room for the family, with a dining area for Christmas dinner. Now we would know how sardines spend the holidays.

And I thought we would have a rough Christmas! By then, it was unimaginable! Sara was deathly sick from the pain medication, and as you might imagine, her nerves were fairly shattered from having to be confined inside a heavy cast. I frankly don't even remember how I got a meal on the table, complete with the Christmas china and silver.

But, as with most families, we all somehow held it together and ate that turkey, opened those gifts, watched that cute baby, and tried to carry on. I suppose the very fact that we were all together somehow created a bond of strength. We remembered how much we still mean to each other. Even though the family structure has changed, the bond is still there, hidden among the tears.

Holidays since that nightmare have gone easier. I am now trying to come to terms within myself to create a whole new Christmas scene that will feel more comfortable for everyone. I am such a traditionalist. For me, I must reinvent this special time of the year to make it, once again, a special and happy family time.

*God of grace and God of mercy, bless our family;*
*our parts and our whole. Bless us as we struggle*

*to find a new understanding of each other and of our future. We love You, God, as we have always loved You and Your special day of birth. Guide us as we continue to seek comfort and balance.*

*To have faith is to step in the direction toward what is believed to be the planned course of our lives. It is obeying God in the unseen areas of our lives.* —BECKY TIRABASSI

Human nature being what it is, men and women from the beginning of time have suffered illness, loneliness, loss, and every sorrow known on earth, just as we do today. Always there has been the challenge of a broken man or woman, kneeling in prayer, reaching out for a God of healing and refuge. The Psalms often reflect that cry:

*Turn your ear to me, come quickly to my rescue; be my rock of refuge, a strong fortress to save me.*
Psalm 31:2

*Hear my cry, O God; listen to my prayer. From the ends of the earth I call to you, I call as my heart grows faint; lead me to the rock that is higher than I.*
Psalm 61:1–2

*In my distress I called to the LORD; I cried to my God for help. From his temple he heard my voice; my cry came before him, into his ears.*
Psalm 18:6

The prayers of darkness in the book of Psalms don't try to gloss over the pain and fear as the individual longs for refuge. There is no offer of quick and easy answers to the suffering. Instead we get true and honest expressions of the struggle to reach God. David again and again begs God to take away his suffering and restore him to wholeness. Jesus later used the words of these same psalms to voice His agony and suffering.

In this way, we know Jesus understands our darkness, suffers with us, and walks with us in the valley of deep despair. That is the greatest comfort of the book of Psalms. It never promises a release of suffering, but it gives us a companion who will go through the darkness with us.

*The LORD is my shepherd, I shall not be in want.*
*He makes me lie down in green pastures,*
*he leads me beside quiet waters,*
*he restores my soul.*
*He guides me in paths of righteousness*
*for his name's sake.*
*Even though I walk*
*through the valley of the shadow of death,*
*I will fear no evil,*
*for you are with me;*
*your rod and your staff,*
*they comfort me.*

Psalm 23:1–4

God has entered into our suffering through the Spirit to bring us comfort until we can stand again, on our own, in His presence with singing and thanksgiving.

Prayers in the darkness are so memorable because the anguish is so intense, but sharing that darkness is comfort beyond belief. When Sara has her badly broken legs and has to be put to sleep to be put in a body cast, the devastation sweeps over us in a way you can't imagine. Every night for the first weeks, she and I arrange ourselves so we can hold hands throughout the night. Touching each other brings strength to us both. Every so often, Sara will cry out, "Mother, are you still there? Hold my hand tighter, talk to me. I need to know you are still there."

That's what happens in the psalms. These prayers in the darkness hold our hand until we can see His face in the morning.

*Lord, teach us to pray through the darkness of the soul and in the pain of our physical suffering. Help us to feel Your grace and feel Your presence as You walk beside us. Increase our faith to know You better. Forgive our weakness and lack of courage in the darkness.*

*When trouble comes, the storm is often so severe
that it bends us to the help that is at hand.*

—RICHARD EXLEY

$\mathcal{I}$ still remember the night Rosemary and Mike came to our house to tell us their big news. They had called earlier and asked to come over after supper with something exciting to share. We waited. We had been friends with Rosemary and Mike for years, even lived down the street from them for a few years. They were fun to be with and anytime they threw a party, the invitations were coveted. They just seemed to attract fun people.

So when they came to tell us their news, we were not surprised that they had decided to leave the corporate world and open a small business. As they explained, life was just too short to let your creativity go to waste—they had always wanted to try their hand in business, and this seemed to be a good time to start.

What we didn't know at the time was that this was not wholly their own choice. Mike had been let go from his corporate job with six-months' severance pay. It had not been a happy parting. And, like the rest of us at that time, they were in the "building" stage of their lives: buying a house, raising children, buying cars. There were no savings accounts, no fall-back accounts, no rainy day funds for any of us. *No job* immediately meant *no income*. And six months' salary was hardly much for a family of five. Mike was fifty-four years old and not a great candidate to start a new career.

Rosemary had worked at small, home-based jobs just to make extra money. So she didn't consider herself to be in a position to become the primary family breadwinner. In Rosemary's own words, "I did not stop for a minute and cry over spilled milk, but instead went into overdrive. How were we going to survive? The children did not know their father had been let go from his job and wouldn't for several years."

Opening a small business was the only option they could come up with, even though the plan was laden with high risks—capital, insurance, and a steady income, to name a few. So using their house for collateral, the business was launched. Rosemary worked at the business until 2:00 in the afternoons, then rushed home to teach piano lessons until 8:00 at night.

As the months progressed, Rosemary seemed to be carrying the heaviest part of the load. The business was barely breaking even. Mike was frozen; he couldn't think beyond the hour he was living. He was a highly creative person, but maybe not the best at business.

The pressure became too much. After three years, the marriage ended, and the business went under, taking their house with it. Everything was gone. In Rosemary's words, "All I had left was myself, and I could see I would have to totally reinvent me, starting from ground zero."

Rosemary had a marvelous personality, and was strikingly attractive. She was very savvy, very gregarious, very good at talking and being with people, so it was no surprise when a major insurance company approached her for commission sales. With a son in college, and big debts to repay, this seemed to be a good option, although it would be hard to learn a new skill. In Rosemary's words, "As I look back, I have no idea how I was able to make it work. I simply put my head down, worked ten hour days, six days a week, and did not come up for air for three years. I had no life, except work. It wasn't until six or seven years into my practice that I began to see some light at the end of the tunnel."

Rosemary wisely went to counseling. The loss of a home, a marriage, and a business all in a short amount of time was just too much. Rosemary reported incredible anger. Two years with a good counselor helped reduce these intense feelings, but did not erase them completely. Even now, constant health problems are daily reminders of the difficult path Rosemary has traveled.

In her words, "The key to my survival was determining what had to be done and doing it! None of this 'poor me' stuff! Was it easy? Absolutely not, but I choose to only look forward and do whatever was necessary to successfully reinvent myself. To survive the traumas that life may bring requires absolute belief in yourself and surrounding yourself with others who believe in you as well. That was seventeen years ago. My children are now happily married, and I have four precious grandchildren. My insurance practice has provided me with a financial safety net. Is my life now a bed of roses? Far from it, but continuing to totally believe in myself gives me purpose, direction, and much joy."

*The LORD will guide you always; he will satisfy your needs in a sun-scorched land and will strengthen your frame. You will be like a well-watered garden, like a spring whose waters never fail.*

Isaiah 58:11

*There is a vast difference between success at twenty-five and success at sixty. At sixty, nobody envies you. Instead, everybody rejoices generously, sincerely, in your good fortune.*

—MARIE DRESSLER (1873–1934)

Probably we've mentioned this before, but it's getting to be "that" time of year again, and I'm excited! Football!

I'm not sure how the rumor got started that women don't like football. Maybe some women don't understand football. And I'll admit I have a lot to learn, but I absolutely *love* football. I love the strategy, I love watching the skill of a well executed play. I love the surprises of an unexpected interception. Well, I could go on, but you get the point.

Last weekend, we saw some of our Tennessee Titans out eating lunch. When you see them on the football field along with all their teammates, you don't realize the size of those fellows. But in a small restaurant, alongside ordinary people, those guys were huge—the size of brick walls! But they are real teddy bears inside. They stopped and talked to us and acted like we were important friends.

As we get closer to the opening of the season, the newspaper is loaded with stories, some from the coaches explaining what we have in store for the season. And, of course, one of the coaching strategies is to sound so big, so bad, and so confident that you intimidate the opposition before you ever set foot on the field.

The game plan almost always calls for taking charge of the game—offensive plays that keep the other team in a state of *reaction*. The announcers always play this strategy up by saying things like, "That quarterback just took possession of this game! He owns it now!" Naturally. If that is *your* team, that's an exciting time.

Now, if you are talking about *life*, it's the same story. When you make a plan, and take charge of the decisions affecting your own life outcomes, you become empowered, productive, and happy. The opposite occurs when you are being forced to live on someone else's terms and are constantly in a state of defense. Let me just say that when the defensive team is on the field, they are only there for one reason— to regain control of the ball, and thus regain control of the game.

For example, Raylene worked for an upscale clothing boutique. She was young, vivacious, and good at what she did. But she worked for an owner who felt very threatened by Raylene's good rapport with the customers. It was a challenge every day for Raylene to get through the day. The owner didn't like the ways Raylene displayed the clothes. She questioned the sales that Raylene made. She constantly criticized (but called it "evaluation").

Raylene felt she was constantly having to defend herself against needless harassment. She was certainly not in control of the game, and it was miserable for both women to try to work together. Raylene could see she would never "win" with a game plan that was constantly one defensive reaction after another.

One day Raylene had a long talk with the owner to discuss how this feeling of impasse was beginning to affect her life. She explained her feelings of inadequacy and her desire to be more a part of a team in the retail business.

The owner was equally articulate, explaining she didn't feel comfortable relinquishing one iota of initiative to Raylene. She admitted to feeling jealous because she thought Raylene was trying to "steal" the best customers. The owner said if this was not the working atmosphere Raylene wanted, then she would need to leave.

And leave, she did. Raylene went to work for a large department store in our city. Because of her experience, she quickly worked up to department manager, helping with displays and attracting her own customers. She could now execute her own game plan and feel she was in control of her own life.

Loss of control over your own life plan is *so* stressful. That's one of the reasons it is so nerve-wracking to be in the hospital, or in a confining illness at home; you forfeit so much control. And that is, of course, why some of our older seniors get so obstinate and hard to deal with; they are losing control of their personal choices and that is really scary.

Design your life's game plan and let life respond to the plays *you* call. Be the quarterback, not a defensive lineman.

*Make it your ambition to lead a quiet life, to mind your own business and to work with your hands, just as we told you, so that your daily life may win the respect of outsiders and so that you will not be dependent on anybody.*
1 Thessalonians 4:11

*What the sun is to the day, what the moon is to the night, what the dew is to the flower, Jesus Christ is to us.* —CHARLES SPURGEON

My days are so fast paced and so full of people that the time just flies by. When I start a new week on Monday morning, sometimes it is late Wednesday before I have time to take a deep breath. I spend my days as director of a bustling and energetic senior activities center.

Recently, I decided to take a little count of just how many different people I come into contact with during a day. Starting with the four to six folks I meet in the elevator while leaving my building, then the doorman, the manager, and the maintenance man, I'm up to about eight folks before I even get to the car.

Then I start adding up the people at work. We have staff and program directors in about twelve different senior initiatives. Then the seniors start coming in. Sometimes up to seventy or eighty a day. Not counting the phone calls, I easily come into contact with a hundred or so folks a day.

Aside from my "no wonder I'm tired" statement, my real point in all of this is to ask myself, *What kind of human conditions have I come across in a day? How many of those seventy-five or so people were hurting and really could have used a boost from me?* I know a lot of my seniors were experiencing physical pain and may not have been feeling well.

And I wonder how many had a happy story to tell and needed someone to listen. When seniors live alone, they desperately need someone to hear their day's events. How many hadn't had a hug in days and would appreciate a little extra attention?

I am humbled when I think of how many opportunities God sends my way every day. I think about the crowds that followed Jesus, each separate individual waiting for a word from the Teacher. And then I think how He had such an uncanny ability to see and know who needed Him the most.

One of our senior men took his own life last year. We grieved and secretly wondered, if we had had *one more* conversation with him, or listened to *one more* story, or engaged him in *one more* activity, would it have saved his life? Could we have helped him want to continue to be among us? We'll never know. But it gave us a long pause.

The responsibility we hold in our hands every day is awesome. I could be the only person who stops and cares for someone during that day. As Christians, we have the words, we have the glow, we have the message to engage dozens of folks a day. Touching their lives, touching their souls, and passing along the love and acceptance that only God can give. I must become more aware of the needs around me!

At the end of this day, I'll never know if I was effective. I'll never know if I did all God needed me to do. I may never realize the one touch I gave that made all the difference to one person. The job is so overwhelming. But I am grateful for the opportunities.

And the strangest thing—I don't give away half what I get back.

*Dear Lord, help me to see people as You would see people. Help me to be more aware of the hurts and needs that You send my way everyday. Help* me to know the words of comfort and solace that You would have me give. Lord, You have given me so much, increase my awareness to give back, constantly engaging people in the kingdom.

*Life has given me of its best—*
*Laughter and weeping, labour and rest,*
*Little of gold, but lots of fun;*
*Shall I then sigh that all is done?*

—NORAH M. HOLLAND (1876–1925)

*S*top reading for a minute and just listen. What do you hear? The sounds of your family moving through the house? The sounds of the day or evening, cars, neighbors coming and going? Do you hear God? Did you hear Him speaking throughout the day? Some random act of goodness from a source you least expected? A thoughtful word?

Or did you experience the absence of those things, but you survived anyway, secure in the knowledge of God's care? That was God speaking, too.

There are no days so ordinary that God is not present in the hours and the minutes—He is usually hidden, always leaving you room to choose to hear Him or not.

It's true. Sometimes God comes to us in burning bushes, in floods, in great winds. But mostly God comes to us one-on-one, in our small personal encounters. He speaks into our daily minutes.

Listen to what your life is saying. In the good times and happy times, God is there, enjoying His creatures in their gladness. In the boredom and the pain and the nothingness come equally key moments of hearing God. In the most humdrum moments, God is still there.

What a glorious mystery is this life! A constant

challenge to bridge the gap between the language of the Spirit and the world of the physical—God and you, with arms reaching, communicating through events, through harmonies and crises of experiences. God making Himself known in a hundred ways.

Do you ever wonder why God doesn't just send an e-mail or write His words in the clouds or speak audibly so that your ears can hear Him? His messages always seem veiled, so subtle that if I don't watch and listen carefully, I miss Him completely. Why?

I think it has to do with my freedom as His child. I am free to hear, or not to hear. His meaning is for me alone. It will have meaning for me only as I search for Him and learn to recognize His voice.

God speaks even in the most obscure moments. Even the in-between moments belong to Him. When I don't want to hear, or when I'm afraid to hear, or just at the moment I think God is no longer there, He speaks. Listening for God and hearing His message comes with practice. It takes time to develop this skill, to develop your companionship with Him to the point you can listen with an understanding heart.

Listen for Him in the rustling grass, listen to Him in the sound of a child's voice, hear Him in the song of a bird, or in the whisper of a breeze. Hear Him in the turn of the key in the lock, listen to Him in the loving words greeting you. The Incarnate Word of grace coming to you when you least expect it. Listen.

> *. . . the sheep listen to his voice. He calls his own sheep by name and leads them out. When he has brought out all his own, he goes on ahead of them, and his sheep follow him because they know his voice.*
>
> John 10:3–4

*Life's an awfully lonesome affair. . . . You come into the world alone and you go out of the world alone yet it seems to me you are more alone while living than even going and coming.*

—EMILY CARR (1871–1945)

*C*ooking an elephant—this old adage just keeps coming up in my life. And if you have a busy or complicated life, it probably is meaningful to you too.

As soon as I sign a contract to write a book, the first emotion I feel and must fight off is panic. *Eighty-seven thousand words by when? I can't do it! That's too much. Too hard. I'll never make it!* If I let that thought-pattern anchor itself in my heart and mind, it would become truth, and my attitude would be so defeated, there would never be a book.

So I've learned, *Step one: you have to cut that elephant into small pieces.* There isn't a job out there that can't be handled if you are willing to break it down into manageable tasks.

I have heard runners or cyclists say the same thing. If they looked at the whole twenty-five-mile course from the starting line, the defeat would be immediate! But if they begin the race and look for the *first* mile marker, then run toward it, the race is off to a good start.

With writing, there is a quirky trick to beginning. I have found that I *circle* like a buzzard for some time. I buy tablets of paper, then stack the tablets just so. I rearrange the lighting. Then I leave to go get more paper or pens. I assemble research books, then rearrange research books. I move the tablets over a few inches and then get the computer set up. You might think that this is very unproductive behavior. But it is part of the dance, and I can't put the first word on paper without it.

*Step two: start cooking the elephant.* Take that first step. No matter how small the step may be, just get started.

At some point, I am faced with sitting down and actually coming in contact with the first blank sheet of paper. Now this is a very tricky step. If the paper stays blank for more than two minutes, the entire dance begins all over again. That wastes more time and I don't want that to happen. So the key is to get *something* on that paper within 120 seconds. Even if it is a sentence that never gets used, I must put some writing on that white paper. And, that's it, I'm off and running.

*Step three: set your cooking timer.* Set small, incremental deadlines with plenty of rewards. When writing, I divide the time and divide the words until I have small goals set for every two weeks or so. Sometimes I even play silly games, like setting smaller goals, knowing I can probably *exceed* those goals early on. My confidence gets a boost and I'm off to the finish line. Keeping my outlook up and positive is 90 percent of the game.

When I reach a goal, and exceed a two-week marker, there are big rewards: like getting to spend the day with two-year-old Abigail, or a small shopping splurge, or a trip to Dairy Queen. Well-met goals are richly rewarded along the way.

*Step four: keep the fire going at a steady pace.* Don't start fast and furiously. Start slow. Build the pace to a comfortable stride and keep putting one foot in front of the other.

I suggested this four-step scheme to a precious friend of mine. She was facing the chore of finding long-term care for her mother, who was bedridden and needed constant supervision. The thought of putting her in a nursing home was so overwhelming that she could not come to grips with the decision. So we sat down and broke the decision up into small steps.

First, we visited various facilities. That part was not so bad, so we got a little reward for meeting that goal.

Then we made a chart of the different kinds of care available and met with social workers at three of the facilities to get feedback and suggestions. We considered this a big accomplishment deserving of another little reward.

Next we took Mama to visit the nursing home. We didn't look at the time frame as "the rest of her life." We set small goals. If Mama could manage for just two weeks, my friend would have a family get-together at the facility, and Mama would get a chance to see everyone. Then we would go for a four-week goal, with a reward at the end of the month.

You can ease into a difficult situation slowly, step-by-step. A steady, persistent rhythm wins the race every time. And a well-thought-out schedule will have that elephant cut up and roasted to perfection in no time.

But the best part of all is standing at the end of a big task, looking back over the course, and thinking, "Wow! Look what I did!"

*Well done, good and faithful servant! You have been faithful with a few things; I will put you in charge of many things. Come and share your master's happiness!*

Matthew 25:21

# ENERGY BOOST

## HE SAID—SHE SAID

*The secret to ridding yourself of a root of bitterness is to forgive and release those who have deeply wounded you.* —LISA BEVERE

We are all different. We have different interests, different priorities, different goals, and different ways we live our lives. We each see the world from different points of view. And that's a good thing. It makes the world go round. It fills our lives with color and interest and opens up new and exciting opportunities. I am so thankful that the world is not made up of people just like me.

As long as I can *celebrate* these differences and recognize the world to be a better place because we are all different, life is good. It is harmonious. It works.

But what if my goals conflict with your goals? What if we both want the same toy at the same time? What if the way you eat gets on my last nerve? What if your spending habits drive me crazy? What if your noisy habit is zapping all of my energy?

Oops! Our differences are no longer lovely ways to make the world a fascinating place to live. Our differences are causing trouble, and my idea of a solution is for you to stop *your* way and begin doing things *my* way. Now our differences have escalated into outright conflict with a big confrontation looming.

Is there a point of no return? Could be. And it is exactly at this point that the battle lines are drawn, and the war is on. Whether we are talking about relationships between a husband and wife, a parent and child, two neighbors, a boss and employee, or some other relationship, the principle is the same. We need to stop right now, at this point, and change the way we're looking at our differences.

Of course, conflict is a part of human nature. I realize that. Everyone wants his or her own way and thinks that way is the right way. I see it demonstrated often with young children, at an age when human beings first learn about conflict—a couple of two year olds fighting over a toy. Each child has an immediate solution in mind: "Give me the toy." Conflict resolved. It's a win-lose solution.

Adults do the same thing. When differences turn into conflict, each party has a solution already mapped out that makes him or her the *winner*. "You do what I want, conflict resolved." And neither party will negotiate. One person wins, one person loses, and a big chunk of trust falls off the relationship.

So, what to do? I have had to learn how to get along with all kinds of people. Along the way, I gleaned a few tips that helped me in conflict management.

1. First, when a conflict arises, I discuss my *interests,* not my *solutions*. Keep your options open until all the points have been put on the table. I work at focusing on being flexible in my

discussion, *without rushing to a conclusion of my own making.*

2. Use the "why" question when you can. *Why* do you feel that way? *Why* do you think we need to buy that? What are the advantages to moving in that direction? This keeps everyone's options open and lets the other person know that I am still open to seeing the other side of the question.

3. And most important—I always try to *listen* with an open mind. It doesn't work to say, "You can state your opinion, but my mind is made up." Or "There is nothing to discuss. I already know what is best." Or "You are so wrong about that, just as wrong as you can be." These statements shut down understanding.

I listen to both sides of the question and to my own statements in light of the other person's feelings. Be willing to cooperate. This is, of course, difficult to do in the parent/child conflict. Sometimes both parties are so locked into a predetermined solution that a compromise is almost impossible. But if both parties will look at all possibilities and realize that no one will get *everything* they want, but both parent and child can get *some* of what they want, it will be worth the effort to find this middle ground.

The process of working through a conflict builds trust, healthy communication, and solid, stable relationships. In relationships or groups where members are *not* allowed to talk about differences of opinion, there is usually a low trust level and always a feeling of win–lose. In these relationships the differences rarely remain differences. Instead, any difference of conviction quickly escalates into open conflict and confrontation where there will be a guaranteed loser.

Conflict that is handled in a healthy, wholesome way can be very good for a relationship. It is an opportunity to make changes that are needed. It can turn a bad situation into something good. It can lead to better understanding between partners. It can change a behavior. And it can create open communication patterns.

God made us in such wonderful ways. He gave us minds and emotions and the ability to love and be loved. And He made the world a colorful, interesting place to live. Then He set us free to live and let live. In this kind of a world we don't always get things just like we want them to be. We can't have all the toys all the time. And we can't be right all the time. But we can always work together for the good of a win-win solution, through building relationships that foster trust and respect for one another.

*Even in darkness light dawns for the upright, for the gracious and compassionate and righteous woman. Good will come to her who is generous and lends freely, who conducts her affairs with justice. Surely she will never be shaken; a righteous woman will be remembered forever.*
Paraphrased from Psalm 112:4–6

# LET'S DO LUNCH!

*Eating is not merely a material pleasure. Eating well gives a spectacular joy to life and contributes immensely to goodwill and happy companionship! It is of great importance to the morale.*

—ELSA SCHIAPARELLI (1896–1973)

*A* friend just called to see about going to lunch next week. I haven't seen her in ages, and I'm so glad she called. By all means, we'll do lunch. How about Thursday? This morning, there's a breakfast meeting to plan a fundraiser. Tomorrow night, dinner with Liz—we need to catch up on grandchildren stories. It's amazing how much of my life centers around eating with friends. Three meals a day—three opportunities for socializing.

Jesus used this plan too—eating and socializing. Remember a little impromptu lunchtime over at Zaccheus' place? Sometimes He went to the big houses and ate with the prominent Pharisees. He had a picnic or two when the teaching went long. He enjoyed a wedding feast and a few little drop-in suppers at Mary and Martha's place. After all without a kitchen of His own, Jesus obviously had to depend on friends for meals here and there.

Table fellowship was important to Jesus, but in a way that we can hardly imagine. Our social structure today allows us to freely pick and choose with whom we eat and where we eat. We even have the chance to try a wide variety of foods.

For Jesus, this was not true. The dietary laws in His day were rigid. Laws governed what could be eaten, exactly how it had to be prepared, and with whom one could or could not eat. No upstanding Jew would share a morsel of food at a table with a woman, a sinner, a tax collector, the poor, or people with disabilities. Yet Jesus ate at the table with all these people.

The meals Jesus shared reflected His vision of an inclusive community. Jesus chose His mealtimes in the same way He ordered His life—to include women, untouchables, the poor, and the worst sinners. Jesus' table mirrored His message—*the inclusive love of God.*

The world of Jesus' day was a world of sharp and clear boundaries; it was a world of exclusiveness. The religious leaders were the powerful elite, and what kept them in this elite status was the way they could continually exclude others from the "in" group. Narrow minds and copious laws defined a small minority of the righteous. Over six hundred laws were designed to divide and separate the pure from the unclean, Jews from Gentiles, men from women, rich from poor. The outcasts of the communities stood outside the houses of the elite to peer in through the windows and doors watching the festive meals of the rich and righteous.

Into this culture, Jesus came and began taking down the barriers, tearing down the fences, opening the invitation to all people. He ate with sinners. His healing shattered the barriers of the unclean. He touched lepers. He elevated women.

This was radical. It was dangerous. But it is what He was born to do. He brought God's compassion to the table.

The same struggle goes on today. We continually draw lines between the righteous and the unrighteous, the good people and the bad people, the churchgoers and the backsliders. We become exclusive in our doctrine and practice, deciding to include only people of our own likeness.

Anytime our circle is drawn in such a way as to exclude a person, or a group of persons, we have missed the message of God's inclusive love and Jesus' open table of fellowship. When we agree to move beyond the boundaries of culturally generated distinctions, we are truly participating in the fellowship of Jesus' open table.

As the early church grew they seemed to value this inclusive invitation and continued this idea of festive, open meals. They used community meals—covered-dish suppers—in their house churches and invited all to come to Christ.

*You are all sons [and daughters] of God through faith in Christ Jesus, for all of you who were baptized into Christ have clothed yourselves with Christ. There is neither Jew nor Greek, slave nor free, male nor female, for you are all one in Christ Jesus.*

Galatians 3:26–28

*Welcoming your husband home from work....
"Listen to him. You may have a dozen important
things to tell him, but the moment of his arrival is
not the time. Let him talk first—remember, his
topics of conversation are more important than
yours."* —"A GOOD WIFE'S GUIDE," HOUSEKEEPING MONTHLY, 1955

*W*hen I let my Texas roots come out to
play, I listen to country music. I don't mean the new
pop/country sounds of recent years. I like the old,
guitar-picking, foot-stomping songs of love and
deception and pain. Loretta Lynn, Johnny Cash,
and Waylon Jennings belted these themes with heart
and gusto.

Back in the "olden days" of my youth, I remember sitting in a booth at the HiWay Café—a very
local eatery (actually, the *only* eatery) in the small
west Texas town where I went to high school. For a
nickel you could coax the red-and-orange bubbling
jukebox to play the mournful wails of Johnny Cash
strumming and singing, "I Walk the Line" and "Cry,
Cry, Cry." I loved it!

As I think back, there was more Texas flavor in that
one dining room than in the burgers. A rare cross section of folks made themselves at home around the
chrome dining tables and red upholstered booths.
First, the ranchers who were coming into town for
supplies and mail. They spent days and sometimes
weeks in the freeing solitude of their ranches, along
with a few sheep and goats, a couple of ranch hands
and a dozen or so diamondback rattlers. But you bet

your boots, they always stopped by for a big, juicy burger at the HiWay Café before they headed back to the wide open spaces of the ranch.

A second group of folks who put ketchup on their fries at the HiWay Café were the truck drivers. Because we had no Interstate system, the narrow, two-lane highways ran through every small town. This great little cafe was the last stop for many miles in both directions, so if a driver wanted supper, he'd better swing into the HiWay Café. These guys lived on the open road, carrying the country's goods down to Del Rio or west to Alpine and finally, California. A hard life to be sure, but most drivers agreed they wouldn't have it any other way. They loved the freedom of that open road.

Now picture these two rough, tough groups readily sharing the space in the HiWay Café with all us high school kids. It was our "hang out" place after school. And believe it or not, it was like we were all part of the big family of west Texans living life at our own level. A cross section of life where young learned from old, and old remembered what it was like to be young. Each giving and taking from the culture. The ranchers, of course, knew all the kids and were kin to most of them. The truckers were regulars and knew some of the ranchers and some of the kids. And they all seemed to take pleasure from watching us kids feed nickels into that blaring jukebox. After all, we all liked the same kind of music—country, loud, soulful, and real.

I am telling this story so I can talk about my personal jukebox favorite of all times—there is no comparison to it, no song even close in second place—"Don't Fence Me In" sung by that indomitable tunemaster, Willie Nelson. It's raw!

Poignant! And hearing it about 1,002 times in that place, with those people, it made quite an impression on me. I can just smell those *"wide open spaces that I love"* and picture myself in that saddle, riding to the ridge to *"stare at the moon until I lose my senses."* I can *feel* that freedom of the crisp air and big open sky every time I hear that song.

Maybe it's a carryover from my Texas roots, and all the unspoken lessons about living free I learned in that little HiWay Café, or maybe it is just a part of my hardheaded, ornery personality, I'm not sure. But the whole idea of personal freedom and the importance of being able to live life on your own terms seems to me to be worth understanding and talking about.

It's true—I can't stand fences. And I don't like barriers or limits. I have a strong belief that each person should be free to live with responsible personal freedom in the least restrictive environment. And for purposes of our discussion here, every woman should be able to experience a personal freedom that allows her to make choices and live life on her own terms. No barriers, and nothing standing in the way of a woman being all that she can be.

Sometimes it seems that the world is full of folks who have lists a mile long, enumerating what all *can't* be done, *shouldn't* be done, or by all means *never consider* doing.

Mostly these fences are built by persons who are trying, themselves, to maintain control—over a relationship, over a group, over a church, or over a denomination.

And it is true that down through the ages, it seems that women have borne the burden of the most rules, the most limitations, and the most barriers to personal freedom—voting, riding public transportation, working outside the home. Only recently were women allowed on certain golf courses or invited into certain civic clubs.

Happily we are making progress in the public arena. But I am saddened to see so many women still under domination in their personal lives. Lack of personal freedom leads to depression, to physical illness, and even to abuse. Lack of personal freedom keeps women from realizing their full potential as God's children.

Claiming your own autonomy is costly and requires tremendous courage. One is likely to encounter criticism and opposition. But keep in mind that many of the female heroines of today were the rebels of yesterday who took personal freedom very seriously.

Personal freedom is a claim you must make yourself—no one can do it for you, but the process will lead you to stretch and think and grow as a person. And what we claim for ourselves, we must in turn offer to others. By empowering and supporting one another in the Lord's work, all our efforts are clearly magnified and multiplied.

God calls people in different ways. I believe that Jesus repeatedly gave examples and offered teachings that empowered women to participate fully and completely in His kingdom. I feel proud to read of the roles and influence that women had in the early church.

And now, God needs you to be free to live in His way. God loves you. God has a plan for you. God gave you a mind and opportunity to make choices for the good of yourself and others for whom you are responsible. Claim your world without fences and without barriers. Claim your best self.

*Now the Lord is the Spirit, and where the Spirit of the Lord is, there is freedom.*
2 Corinthians 3:17

*A good many women are good tempered simply because it saves the wrinkles coming too soon.*

—Bettina von Hutten (1874–1957)

If you really want to see a person's true colors, find out how she celebrates her birthday. Think about it!

For example, my friend Diane (not her real name) can't stand birthdays. When we mention a birthday coming up, she starts backing up—"Oh, don't even mention birthdays! You know I don't celebrate birthdays anymore. I don't even want to think about it." Poor thing, her self-esteem is all tied up in her perception of perpetual youth. She thinks that as her friends start counting her age, she will have less value. So no mention is allowed, no celebration, no birthday noise at all.

Isn't that sad? Actually this plan rather reflects her life. She is insecure, doubtful of herself, has the feeling that life has passed her by. I sometimes wonder if the cry of "no birthday" isn't a sort of cry for attention, hoping that the more she protests, the more we'll beg and the more attention she will actually receive. I do feel sorry for Diane because whatever her intentions are, it reflects a sad void in her life.

On the opposite end of the scale is my friend Jean (yes, this is her real name). Jean is the ultimate birthday girl. She loves birthdays—hers or anyone else's. She keeps an extensive calendar of everyone's birthday. She makes a point of giving lots of spotlight time, along with thoughtful gifts and cards, to everyone on her list. And guess what happens when it is *her* birthday? You guessed it. Everyone gets excited about her special day because she is a good gift receiver. Her office looks like Christmas morning. She "holds court" all day, receiving well-wishers, lunches, gifts from everyone.

This plan, too, reflects exactly who Jean is. Jean loves life, loves to shop, loves to give, and loves people. She is constantly planning meals, events, and ways to enjoy her friends. So, in turn, people love Jean back.

For my thirty-year-old Sara, birthdays are beginning to remind her that adult birthdays may not be quite as much fun as childhood birthdays. When she was young, we put our best creative efforts into her birthdays. While most of her friends were having skating parties and swimming parties, we had to plan parties that would be deliciously fun, but doable for the honoree who used wheels.

One year we took all of her friends downtown to eat in Nashville's new revolving restaurant. (It was a new thing to most of them.) We chose to go at lunchtime so that it didn't take our entire life savings, and it was a big-hit birthday party with the ten-year-old girls.

One year, conveniently, one of Sara's brothers was dating a darling girl who had a part-time job at a cosmetic counter. Perfect! We invited her to do a make-up party complete with lots of free samples. For twelve year olds, that too, was a hit and gave Sara plenty of time in the spotlight before, during, and after the party.

Now Sara thinks the birthday parade is just a little too slow for grown-ups. Of course, I assure her I'm still available, with party supplies in hand, to plan the big 3-0 party. But she assures me that her friends will take care of the plans. Moms don't plan grown-up parties.

My attitude about birthdays is different yet. I love birthdays. And, if I anticipate that my own birthday celebration is looking a little low-key, I'm not against jumping right in and planning my own party, plus buying myself a very fun surprise. Do I think this is a selfish thing to do? Heck no! I am a good giver of gifts, I plan good things for others, and when it is my spotlight day, I figure I'm worth it.

Another favorite action I engage in on my birthday is to send notes, and sometimes flowers, to people who have been especially meaningful to me during the year. I celebrate my day by celebrating the people who make my life good. You know, like those acceptance speeches on awards shows. While I'm enjoying the spotlight, "I'd like to take this opportunity to thank . . . "

So stand in that spotlight, girl! Stand tall, right in the middle of that light, and *enjoy.* You deserve every minute. Never get too old to have birthdays. They don't come that often—only once a year! And birthdays are a lot better than the alternative.

Celebrate every minute of your wonderful life. It's not a selfish thing to do—it's a good thing, a human thing, a be-true-to-yourself thing.

*Satisfy us in the morning with your unfailing love, that we may sing for joy and be glad all our days.*

Psalm 90:14

# CHANGE IS IN THE AIR

*The earth has rolled around again and harvest
time is here,
The glory of the seasons and the crown of all the
year.* —CAROLYN WELLS (1869–1942)

There's a change coming. A big change. I can feel it in the air. It's subtle so far, but it's there! And I am so excited—my most favorite time of the year. Fall's coming!

The trees are turning dark, dark green—the color that comes just before they burst into red, orange, and gold. There's just a tinge of crispness in the air—a hint of things to come.

I'm always thankful for the passage of August. Part of that feeling dates back to when the children were young and in school. By August the fun had worn off of summer, and everyone was bored and fighting and tired of being at loose ends. Even before August begins, the heat and humidity have worn me out; it is such an effort to deal with summer temperatures, with the air conditioning constantly running full blast.

Maybe that's why fall is so special. Fall brings a feeling of renewal for me. There is always an excitement about the beginning of school. New school supplies, new shoes, new backpacks. I remember how much fun we had getting three kids ready for new classes. (But by the time we actually got ready, I felt like meeting those school buses with a brass band!)

The fall rituals are as comforting as Mama's kitchen. At the first cold snap I get out the bread pans and my twenty-year-old cookbook and bake pumpkin bread. The smells of those spices just scream, "Home, hearth, and family." I bake enough for a list of friends and neighbors—some loaves with raisins and nuts, and some loaves without, for my silly kids who still don't like foods that are "mixed up."

Then we can all hardly wait for the day we declare *Pumpkin Buying Day*. We head for Earl's vegetable stand, the place where we have bought pumpkins since Chase was a baby. Now we take his babies and shop just as carefully for the right size and shape. We get enough big and little pumpkins for all our households and enough for the babies to hold and play with. Money is no object when we're buying the fall pumpkins.

Of course, certain foods go along with all these fall traditions. The first big pot of vegetable soup made with Mother's recipe. The first big pot of two-alarm chili. It just all falls (no pun intended) into place like a giant seasonal puzzle. Immediately I feel energized, my spirits lift, and my creativity soars.

Actually the same thing happens as we approach winter. The big holiday season is like ending the year with a gala party where everyone celebrates for a month. The day after Thanksgiving, all the pumpkins go away and Christmas comes out. Every day of December has its rituals, its favorite foods, its smells, and its good times.

Then comes January, when we can put away all the seasonal things, clean house, and get out the snuggle blankets. The cold is so refreshing and purifying. The world goes into hibernation. It's strange, but no matter how busy my January schedule is, I still feel like it is a restful, sleepy, hibernating time.

And next comes beautiful, exhilarating spring. The tiny crocus bulbs signal new life, and immediately I change the candles to a spring scent and run out to dig in the earth. Out comes the rabbit-and-carrot collection and plans begin for a big Easter celebration with the special green jello salad that everyone loves. It is a wonderful resurrection time in every sense of the word.

Every season is special, with its own clothes, colors, food, and traditions. It's our path of connecting with creation. It's a primitive thing really—celebrating life the way it was meant to be, before we had air conditioning and central heating.

Ecclesiastes has the most poetic description: *"There is a time for everything, and a season for every activity under heaven" (3:1)*. It's a beautiful, sacred, divine plan—a way to be in balance, in harmony with nature, God's creation.

*One's purpose in life doesn't depend on understanding God's plan, but how we respond to a tough circumstance right now, this day, this instant.* —JONI EARECKSON TADA

The signs were all there. Donna was a nervous type anyway, but we all noticed that she acted more afraid than usual. To tell you the truth, my suspicious nature had already led me to feel very cautious around her friend Rick. And with Donna's nervous attitude when she was with him, I was wondering what might be going on. He was a little bizarre by my standards, always talking in circles and speaking with such deliberate confidence that it was close to being obnoxious.

Whenever he barked, Donna jumped. When she was in a group without him, she would nervously look at her watch with the constant reminder, "Rick doesn't like me to be late!"

Then one day she showed up for lunch with her arm in a sling. We all inquired about the injury. Her nervousness was obvious, and the explanation was vague. "Oh it's just a little accident. It's okay. He didn't mean anything by it."

Wrong answer. My suspicions grew. Donna was being abused. But what could I do?

When Rick showed up with Donna, his verbal abuse escalated. He berated her, he called her dumb, and soon we seldom saw either one of them in group events. When Donna did appear, she always wore long-sleeved blouses or blouses with high necks.

One night at a Christmas party, it all came to a head. Rick arrived at the party having already had too much to drink. Donna was a wreck. She was frantically trying to keep Rick under control as well as assure everyone else that all was well. During the course of the evening, Donna and Rick were dancing. At one point, Rick grabbed Donna's arm, twisted it behind her, hit her in the face, and yelled, "You idiot, you're still not doing it right! Do what I say, or you're going to be sorry!"

The party fell to a hush. Did we hear what we thought we heard? Rick was just sober enough to realize what he had done in front of fifty people. Donna was so scared, I thought she would faint. A couple of the guys tried to take Rick aside to talk, but he was in no condition to be reasoned with. The couple left soon after.

The following week, I called Donna and gently inquired if she was all right. She insisted she was fine and said, "I know what you're calling about. But you need not worry. Rick had to do that the other night. He wants only the best for me, and that's the only way he can teach me, so I can learn to dance correctly."

I was stunned that anyone would, or could, come up with reasoning such as that. I suggested that she rethink that scene. No one has to be taught using pain and threats and bullying. I assumed that Rick was within hearing distance because Donna was short and unyielding in her defense of him.

I was heartbroken, because I could only imagine what was going on. They dropped out of the social circle and were seldom seen in public. Other friends tried to intervene, all to no avail.

Abuse of a spouse or girlfriend is far more prevalent than you would ever think. If it is blatant enough to look suspicious, it is probably true. And not just physical abuse, but verbal and emotional abuse also.

If someone is treating you as less than an equal, you don't have to stand for it. Put-downs, intimidation, threats, and control are all beginning stages of abuse. It may not move beyond that, but these things are enough.

A husband who maintains complete control of the family's finances, never allowing the wife to know what the money situations even are, is not treating his marriage partner fairly.

A spouse who expects to be waited on hand and foot, who is a guest in his own home, is not building his marriage in a fair way.

A husband who exercises control to the point of limiting phone calls and limiting his wife's freedom to come and go is overstepping the boundaries of a marriage contract.

Name calling, snide remarks, and constant criticism are all things that keep a woman under "control" and are a form of abuse.

Of course, hitting, twisting arms, or any threat of such is out of the question.

Call a marriage counselor immediately. Or talk to your minister. You do not have to spend your life under someone's control. Liberate yourself. Set new ground rules. Don't give your power and control away. God loves you as a free and independent woman. Find someone to help!

*And the peace of God, which transcends all understanding, will guard your hearts and your minds in Christ Jesus.*

Philippians 4:7

# LIVE WITH PANACHE

*The hardest habit of all to break*
*Is the terrible habit of happiness.*

—THEODOSIA GARRISON (1874–1944)

*T*here are times when it is just plain fun to impress, to dazzle, to do something memorable. This is especially important if you are in sales, or if you want to meet someone new, or if you are the new person in a group or on a committee.

Then there are times when I need to feel extra-special for myself. When emerging from my wilderness exile, I found that I needed an outward boost to my self-concept, an edge to bolster my courage, a kind of social kick-start. In my words, I needed *panache!* I wanted to do the unexpected, wear something marvelous, have a distinctive party. I felt a need to reestablish myself as a social person.

It starts with appearance. Always dress as if you were meeting your dream date. Find out what everyone else is wearing, then wear something slightly different. Put yourself together—all together, like my friend Dorothy. Everything she does, she accomplishes with *panache*. When she enters a room, she is immediately noticed. For one thing, she is always dressed impeccably, usually wearing something a little different. Beautifully matched outfits, always with a matching neck scarf. She stops and speaks to everyone in the room personally. She is happy and magnetic.

You can also accomplish *panache* by doing the unexpected. Instead of giving a party, invite your guests to a *soiree*. It's the same thing, but doesn't it sound special? Send invitations with glitter in the envelope, or sealing wax and ribbons on the outside. Have a costume party, or a party in an unusual location. I recently attended an elegant candlelight wedding dinner in a barn. You might use a hundred votive candles and have dinner at a park.

Do the unexpected, wear something spectacular, excel at something few people can do. All it takes is imagination and desire. Can you play tunes on the rims of water glasses? Do you grow orchids? Can you identify unusual birds? Or fold origami? Learn to do something unusual.

There is a saying, "It only costs a little more to go first class!" Sometimes this is true. If you can do with fewer possessions, really go for *panache* with what you do buy. This would be true with jewelry, clothes, or furnishings. I would rather have one really striking piece of jewelry than five pieces of so-so accessories. Liz, my dear friend, does this. Her clothes are simple and stylish. She tops off her outfits with a sizable or unusual necklace, and it is always stunning. Craft fairs and art shows are usually good places to pick up outstanding neckpieces.

Act enthusiastic. Even if you are shy, try to enter into groups and activities with gusto. Don't overdo, but be ready to enjoy opportunities. Be a part of the action. That's panache. However, don't mistake panache with "showing out." Panache is accomplished with a great deal of sophistication and finesse.

Go the second and third mile on anything you do. If you have guests for dinner, use the best china. Create a dinning experience. Use candles and fresh flowers. Make it special. In fact, develop a fetish for fresh flowers—on your desk, in your office, at home, wherever. *Real panache!*

Always go for quality. If a job has your name on it, do it better than it has ever been done before. Do it quicker. If you're making a report, illustrate your points in a handout or on charts. Make it unique. Make it unforgettable.

If "living well is the best revenge," then enjoy a little harmless revenge. I'm not talking about living beyond your means or buying luxuries that are outside your finances. But I am saying invest in a little luxury when you can. Consider yourself worthy of the good life. Not in a bragging, selfish way, but in a manner of enjoying a few nice things.

If you are reclaiming yourself from some lost time, reenter life like Carol Channing in *Hello, Dolly!* Think of yourself entering a room with chorus singing behind you in full voice, "It's good to have you back where you belong." That scene was the perfect illustration of panache. And like Carol Channing, not only will you feel sensational, you will be remembered.

*All the days of the oppressed are wretched, but the cheerful heart has a continual feast.*
                                    Proverbs 15:15

# WAKE-UP CALL—
## YOU NEED A VACATION

*I knew my life was severely out of balance, even though I wasn't doing bad things; it was a life filled with wonderful and challenging things I thought I'd always wanted. But it was too much and I was being crushed by it.*

—NANCI CARMICHAEL

*W*hy is it so forbidding to *stop* doing things when you need to? Why do we work and work and continue long past the time when we need to stop and schedule in some "me" time?

Twice I have had wake-up calls that were like watching a funny movie of a woman out of control. Both events led me to the nearest travel agent for a vacation.

The first happened in the big eight-story parking garage at my doctor's office. I had a zillion things on my agenda that day. And, of all things, a doctor's appointment that had been on the calendar for six months. I took work to do, because I couldn't afford to waste one minute of time if I had to wait—which was a certainty.

I quickly wound round and round the garage to find a parking place and rushed right in. Sure enough, there was a wait, and the office visit, and yet another discussion with the nice doctor about stress-related problems. "Okay, okay, sure, see ya later!"

I went rushing back to my car. I had just enough time to get to Sara's office to pick her up for lunch, then get her back to her office by 1:30 for a meeting. It was tight, but barring unusual circumstances, we could make it.

As you can guess, an unusual circumstance arose! I lost the car! I was in such a hurry I forgot to notice color codes or numbers or symbol codes, even though those kinds of things were posted everywhere. Was I on the "orange star" floor? Or, no, I think I remember the "green turtle" floor. No. Maybe not.

I starting looking, but grew more panic stricken as I went along. Out of eight floors, where was that car? By now, I was running out of my designated time for this activity, so I called Sara to alert her to making a Plan B for lunch.

Sara is a smart and gifted individual, and when she suggests a solution, it is usually a dandy plan. "Mother, punch the panic button on your key chain and you can locate the car by sound!" Smart girl, that Sara. That's why I was happy to have spent well over $100,000 for her education.

So I headed back to the garage, panic button in hand. Sure enough, I could hear that horn sounding—nice, loud, evenly spaced honks! But from which direction? The horn was echoing, wildly bouncing from one concrete wall to the next, all up and down those eight floors. By now, I expected the Metro Police Department to send ten of it's best men over to check this noise out. But no, not one public servant showed up. Who were those panic buttons suppose to summon, anyway?

My next plan was to walk off and come back at midnight. But by then someone would have had the car with the dead battery towed off. So I had to stick it out.

Thankfully, with a little embarrassing help from total strangers, I found my car and was able to pick back up on my crunch schedule. I actually finished all of my agenda that day, but I decided I could see a long weekend off in my immediate future.

My other wake-up call came in the grocery store years ago. All three kids were sick with the chicken pox. (Yes, all at one time!) I was in dire need of groceries, but I couldn't leave my little dotted children. Finally I was able to obtain the services of a neighbor for one hour. She would sit on one side of the room, and the children were supposed to stay on the other. The best I could hope for under these circumstances was an hour, and that was pressing my luck.

I drove like a wild woman to the supermarket, grabbed a basket, and started ripping through that store, close to twenty miles an hour—me and basket darting in and out of aisle after aisle.

Marathon time, basket full, I headed for the checkout counter. I reached for my purse to pay—it wasn't there! My purse had been stolen out of my basket!

All the weeks of three sick kids came pouring out in tears. "My purse is gone! Someone took my purse!"

The managers assembled slowly, asked a few questions, then announced for shoppers to check that they had the correct shopping cart. I was furious! Shouldn't someone be trying to block the entrances and exits to catch that pirate? For heaven's sake, I watched TV; I knew what you were supposed to do to catch a thief!

At about that time, along came a sweet little granny shopper pushing *my* grocery cart, complete with my purse (untouched), and all the groceries I had selected! In my haste and distraction, I had picked the wrong cart and taken it to checkout.

I tried to smile a little guilty-looking grin, hoping they weren't going to put me on a bus to the funny farm. I dried my tears, checked out, and slowly drove home.

It was a bad scene, but I got a trip to Hawaii out of the deal. My husband, Mancil, was scheduled to go to Hawaii in two weeks for a business trip. We decided that a second ticket wouldn't break the budget and would certainly be a much-needed break for me. Mother (God bless her) agreed to run Chicken Pox Hotel for a week. That vacation was probably one of the most life-saving trips of my life.

When life gets crazy, back off and spend some time refocusing, vacationing, or making some complete change of pace. Scientists talk about inertia of motion. They have discovered that if an object is moving, it has the tendency to continue moving. And if that moving object is a mother, I might add, she keeps moving in circles.

Stop the run, even for an hour's soak in a bubble bath. No little folks outside the door pounding to get in. Take care of *you* before you take care of others, or else you might lose your basket.

*Dear Lord, help me to see myself as one who also needs nurture, and rest, and reprieve. So many people depend on me, it makes it hard to draw lines. I love making life good for others, but help me see my own needs too. Help me in my continual search for balance in my life and in my giving.*

# What Is Old?

Age never ceases to amaze me. There are fifty-five year olds who have declared themselves old, and by George, they are very nearly accurate. They limp around constantly, talking about aches and pains. They dress old and talk about boring subjects, like what life was like twenty years ago.

At the same time I have acquaintances who are seventy-nine and eighty years old. They are soon leaving on a cruise to Australia. They can discuss world events, literature, the latest best-selling book, and they have a ball on the dance floor.

Now, of these three, who is old?

For years, the American Association of Retired Persons (AARP) and various other groups who address aging issues have tried to come up with a term to describe the older population. Are they to be called "seniors," "golden oldies," "prime timers," "retired persons," what? And when should they get the label? Age fifty-five, forty-five, sixty-five, ninety, when?

For what it's worth, I like the term "adult"! No senior to it, just adults of various ages. Generally, around the ages of eighteen to twenty-one, a child legally becomes an adult. But the measurement at the other end of life is determined by attitude and health status, both physical and mental.

In other words, people can make themselves old by adopting old ways, old attitudes, and an old appearance. I've never understood why anyone would do this, but they do. I bet you've noticed it too. Perhaps it garners them a little sympathy or life perks—I don't know.

Poor health is a tricky circumstance. A short-term illness may sidetrack us for a short while, but a debilitating illness can age even the best of us overnight. At this point, one becomes a senior adult, regardless of chronological age.

My plan leaves the bulk of adults, ages fifty-five or over, as just *adults*. Some may be retired, but a lot still work. Many travel. Almost all exercise as often as possible.

We are entering the time in which we will have the healthiest, the most financially stable, the best-educated adults in history. And they are going to be a large and significant group of the overall population.

These folks are already primed to be the most active adults we have seen; they are not ready to age unnecessarily. Many will retire from one job and then start a new business or career. This new breed of adult will be the quintessential volunteer, giving back to the community and to the world.

It will be a case of aging exquisitely. None of this sitting around all day playing checkers and watching TV. Instead these adults over fifty-five will be working, traveling, and using the Internet to do their household chores.

I am not claiming they have found a fountain of youth, and I am not advocating that a sixty-five year old try to look and act forty. In my writings, I have declared that there is nothing more elegant than a woman in the fall or winter of her life, acting and looking her age. This shows a woman in balance with herself and her feelings.

People who are sixty-five today just look and act a lot different than they did fifteen years ago. Women who have it all together, who are still productive, still giving back to their friends and their communities, are not *seniors*. They are *adults*.

You can become a senior anytime you choose. It's easy actually. Make your own health your number-one topic of conversation. Spill a little food on your clothes, but go out anyway. Stop reading the newspaper or watching the news on TV so that you will have very little to talk about. Whine and complain a lot about how good things used to be. This will all work together nicely to create a senior overnight.

But for me, I think I'll just stay an adult. I may add some eccentric touches here and there just to shake things up a bit. But the complaining and whining—I'll leave that to the folks who want to be seniors.

*But do not forget this one thing, dear friends: With the Lord a day is like a thousand years, and a thousand years are like a day.*
2 Peter 3:8

*A courage mightier than the sun—you rose and fought and fighting, won!* —ANGELA MORGAN (1874-1957)

During the spring of last year, Sara was scheduled to attend a business meeting in Washington D.C. She is chairperson of a state committee that gathers with groups from other states on a yearly basis. I get to go along on some of these fun trips. (It comes from knowing the right people.) My role on this trip was a simple one to begin with—just be available to help when needed. But as it turned out, the trip required much more of us both than we ever dreamed.

We arrived at the airport, with tickets in hand, for the two-hour flight to D.C. The secretary had made all the reservations, and we walked in as confident as two women could be. The first hint of trouble came when we were called to board the plane. With hope in our hearts and a sense of adventure, we walked to the gate. And would you believe they boarded that plane directly off the tarmac up a steep flight of stairs! (When is the last time you had to board from the tarmac? I couldn't believe my eyes.) We stood at the bottom of those stairs, looking up—Sara in a two-hundred-pound electric wheelchair and me with an arm full of carry-on luggage. I looked at the airline agents with a big question mark on my face. I said, "How are we supposed to get on this plane?"

With blank looks on their faces, they said, "Oh, can't she walk?" Right then I knew we were in serious trouble.

To make a very long story short, I will mention only the highlights of this memorable trip. The two-and-a-half-hour trip eventually took sixteen hours. The baggage handlers dropped the wheelchair (not with Sara in it, thank goodness) out of the baggage compartment of the plane onto the tarmac, not once, but *twice*—completely disabling all the electric wiring. At one point we were deposited in Philadelphia (nowhere near our destination) with a very useless, mangled wheelchair, all our luggage, no connecting flights, and no airport support.

Hours later, after finally arriving in D.C. well after midnight, the driver of the one accessible van in town had already gone home, and we were stranded at the airport for another hour or two while the hotel tried to locate a driver.

While we waited, there was plenty of time to push the disabled chair with a very weary Sara, plus a cart full of luggage, through the airport to locate a complaint department. Sara and I both tried to maintain a tiny shred of dignity. Without crying we told our story of abuse.

The complaint lady assured us that it was "no big deal—they dropped wheelchairs all the time." I was horrified! In fact, they dropped and disabled so many wheelchairs the airline had their own wheelchair repair department. They would pick up Sara's chair at the hotel the next morning and bring a loaner chair for her to use.

Of course, if you know anything about wheelchairs, they are all different, all measured to certain specifications, and substitute chairs are very difficult to use. But we were desperate. Sara had several calls to make at various offices around the capitol, so we had to take what we could get. We padded the loaner chair with phone books to make the seat high enough. (Sounds comfortable, doesn't it?) Then a couple of pillows at the back, and off we went.

The trip home was less eventful, for which we were thankful. But her wheelchair was almost a total loss, leaving Sara with yet another loaner for six more weeks at home while they ordered parts. When you have to depend on mechanics for your daily living, it leaves you at the mercy of people—sometimes helpful and nice people, sometimes not.

Since Sara's birth thirty years ago, the world has made some wonderful changes for persons with disabilities. I hope that we have been responsible for some of that. I have little or no faith that a commercial airplane will ever be a safe, friendly place for wheelchair users. But I have great faith and hope that the world in general is becoming open and inviting to persons with all kinds of disabilities. More doors are now being opened to folks who need some accommodation to enter the mainstream of society. And believe it or not, churches are some of the most obvious places where people with disabilities still have the least acceptance and accommodation.

These are opportunities for your closest consideration. Do yourself a real favor and introduce yourself and your children to friends who happen to have disabilities. Include children who have disabilities in play groups and family activities. Then make an effort to learn friendly and acceptable language and etiquette.

Here are a few examples of language and etiquette:

- If you wish to speak to a person with a disability, speak to him or her directly, rather than talking *about* him or her to the companion.

- Do not use the term *wheelchair bound*. Instead say, *uses a wheelchair*.

- Remember that words such as *blind, deaf,* and *disabled* are adjectives and should describe the person—that is, people with disabilities, people who are blind, people who are deaf.

- People who use wheelchairs are not necessarily hearing impaired; you don't need to shout.

- Regardless of the disability, remember that people who use wheelchairs are charming individuals with a lot to contribute to society.

So, may I ask you, if you see Sara and me struggling through an airport with a broken wheelchair, please stop to see if we could use a little help. I'll probably hug your neck.

*He who dwells in the shelter of the Most High will rest in the shadow of the Almighty. I will say of the LORD, "He is my refuge and my fortress, my God, in whom I trust."*

Psalm 91:1–2

# THE RUDE HOST AND
# THE UNINVITED GUEST

*I*t must have been such an embarrassing
moment. Simon, the dinner host, was rude and
unthinking to his dinner guest. And he got caught
in the act, right in front of everyone.

A Pharisee named Simon invited Jesus to dinner.
It is hard to know exactly how this event came about
because we don't have a lot of information. I have
often wondered: when Jesus was invited to dinner, did
that include some or all of the disciples? Or did the
others have to scrounge around for some invitations
of their own? I also wonder if these were spur-of-the-
moment invitations or if Simon issued the invitation
well in advance. As a woman, I'm curious about little
details like that. But since men wrote the accounts,
that was not their focus.

When Jesus showed up for dinner, it was the custom for the host to wash the feet of an honored guest
and to anoint his head with perfumed oils at the very
beginning of the evening. It was the very minimum
welcoming tradition in a well-to-do home.

But Mr. Simon forgot his manners. No feet washing, no kiss in greeting, and no anointing. What a
rude host! Did he explain, "Oh gee, we are fresh out
of perfumed oils, hope you don't mind!" Or "My
back is killing me. Sorry about the foot washing!"

Whatever the case, we have to assume that Jesus
was not his honored guest. He must have been invited

as a curiosity. Maybe Simon was just interested to see what this rebel Rabbi was all about.

Of course, Jesus noticed this oversight, and obviously knew what was in Simon's heart. Do we really think we fool God?

The dinner began, and as was the custom in fancy houses, only men were at the table, and they were stretched out on pallets placed around the table. (Can you imagine trying to eat while you are propped up on one elbow?)

Another curious custom also comes into play here. Dining areas were basically open to the street, so that various neighbors and street people could stand around outside the dinner and peer in at the goings-on. Oh yeah, that sounds like fun! The *haves* are all enjoying a good meal, while the *have-nots* are looking on, drooling maybe?

All of a sudden, one of the women from the street walked right in and stood crying before Jesus, with her tears falling on His feet. Then she wiped His feet with her hair and poured perfume on them.

Now we're left with all kinds of questions. Had she known Jesus before? Had He already talked to her, forgiven her, and lifted her to a new life? We don't know. But we do know that the irresistible love of God had touched her life in such a way that she wanted to make a statement of her response to the Lord of her life. We have every reason to believe she was sincere and acting out of her deepest feeling. We know this because what she did risked the anger of Simon and ridicule by the other guests. It also put Jesus at risk of ridicule. And it was an expensive gesture, probably using a big portion of her life savings.

And what was rude Simon's response to this tender scene? He must have rolled his eyes and made a disgusting face, because his thought was, "If Jesus was a prophet, then He would know what a no-good person she is!" Then in his best Pharisee way, he must have felt so righteous. What a good man he was to tolerate such tomfoolery in his own home. And now he had seen Jesus in action—if you could call it that—allowing a streetwalking *woman* to touch His feet!

Just at that moment, Jesus caught Simon in the act of thinking. "Simon," He said, "I came to your home and you offered me no welcome, no courtesy. But this woman has done all the honorable things you omitted."

He gave Simon a short story to illustrate His favor of honest, forgiven people, no matter what their pasts had been. Then He said to the woman, "Your sins are forgiven. Your faith has saved you, go in peace."

Her sins were gone—as if they never happened. In their place was a peace she had never known. Gone was her life on the streets. In its place was obviously a need to serve. Life is never the same after a personal encounter with the Master.

And to think Simon was sitting right there. The same could have been his experience. But his self-righteousness was more of a barrier than all of the woman's sin. He never experienced the saving grace that was his for the asking.

Once again Jesus forgave a sinner, and once again, He tore down the barriers that divided people.

*Therefore, I tell you, her many sins have been forgiven—for she loved much. But he who has been forgiven little loves little.*

Luke 7:47

# ENERGY BOOST

## To Thine Own Self Be True

*In all these things we are more than conquerors through him who loved us.* —ROMANS 8:37

*T*he chapters of this book cannot close without one more commission about the value and importance of knowing yourself, loving yourself, and respecting your needs.

Why this is such a struggle for women, I am not sure, but it has been a point of growth for many of us, most of the time.

Domestication and cultural expectations often force women into service roles—taking care of others—being subservient. To this day, I could no more turn down a request from one of my children than I could fly. And so far as I had strength, I ran a household to near perfection—because that was what was expected. Women are genetically disposed to caring for others. It is that old nurturing thing.

Don't get me wrong; there is absolutely nothing wrong with a woman being a good and happy wife and mother. It is the noblest of callings, and when it is done well, it is beautiful to behold. It is biblical. A family working together in mutual love and respect with a harmony of responsibility is a picture blessed by God and admired by mankind. Families are the foundation of all that is good and holy in our world. Freely and graciously, members of a Christian family share and listen and make allowances for each other—this is a way of balanced submission, shared and interdependent respect for each other's various roles.

But somehow we have an extraordinary habit of taking the best teaching and the best intentions and turning them into the worst results. Many of us have been subjected to such a misconstrued form of biblical submission that we are tempted to reject the teaching all together.

The limits of being subservient are: (1) when submission becomes destructive and a woman is denied her right to personal fulfillment, (2) when it denies the New Testament teaching of respect and love, (3) when it treats a woman as property or chattel, or (4) when the expectation is to submit to an earthly authority by means of manipulation.

Do you see the difference? Earthly submission for the sake of providing better service to an ungrateful household is not spiritual. That's enslavement. When submission is designed to "keep a woman in her place," it becomes destructive and denies human value.

This enslaving submission can occur through a subtle progression. And in one brief, shining moment, you may suddenly realize that you cannot continue to play by the rules you have lived with for so long.

Far from being the act of a selfish, self-centered, midlife woman, it is the bravest, most honest thing you can do—to speak the truth of your heart, to open the door of your own life and live it as fully as you can. This requires a transformation and it can happen in one of three ways.

1. Usually a transformation requires a break from the old life because it is hard to gracefully step into a new role without making some major changes that affect everyone around you. And while this new way of life may feel so right for you, it will not feel so great for people who may have to get up and get the salt for themselves.

2. A transformation to a life of self-affirmation may occur because you have experienced a loss, a grief, or a major upheaval in your life. Sometimes we are forced into a new birth process whether we wanted one or not. A serious illness, a loss, a move, a change in family status—these can precipitate life changes. When this occurs you have to deal with the grief and change alongside the rebuilding, which makes your journey both easier and harder. It is easier because the course of history has changed, and you no longer are governed by how "you've always done it." It is harder because you are dealing with loss and gain at the same time. Pain and loss are not essential for claiming your life, but sometimes it all goes together.

3. Rather than a total life overhaul, this third kind of transformation is like recognizing a lifestyle whose time has come—a time to respond to who you are. This subtle new way of life needs cooperation, understanding, commitment from the people around you; otherwise it is nothing new. It will be just a reshuffling of the same old ways and attitudes.

Somewhere within all of us is the knowledge of our own lives as we would like them to be. And yet, so often we have sold out our opportunities to live those lives and choose instead the lives that others have chosen for us. But you can give birth to yourself. Life is an opportunity for you to contribute love in your own way. Use your strength and energy to live and love fully.

In listening to your own true inner voice, you will become a woman who can serve based on a commitment of loving and giving rather than on an obligation. You can grow, you can become, you can feel respected for who you are. Don't let anyone take this from you.

Only you can hear your life calling, and only you can respond.

*Create in me a pure heart, O God, and renew a steadfast spirit within me. Do not cast me from your presence or take your Holy Spirit from me. Restore to me the joy of your salvation and grant me a willing spirit, to sustain me.*

Psalm 51:10–12

# ON MY WAY—I FOUND ME!

*Trust God that God is doing for you what He has done for zillions of people throughout the world for generations.* —THELMA WELLS

On my way to a new, single lifestyle, guess who I found? ME! I had been gone a long time—hidden among the schedules, the expectations, the building of a family. On most days, it was difficult to find myself.

Really all I knew about myself was what was reflected back to me from the people around me. I was the wife who decorated the house for wonderful family events and had a good dinner on the table every night at 6:00, the mother who fixed broken shoelaces and hunted for lost puppies. I was the dutiful daughter and the tireless volunteer. I was the grocery buyer, the maker of little dresses, the repair seamstress for band uniforms, the baker of pound cakes for teachers. I could buy crayons and coloring books and make broken legs feel better. I could drive a car in three directions at once to get to ball practice, music lessons, and a church meeting.

Those were good years—rich in reward and building of memories. How I loved and was loved. Those were also challenging years—raising two sons was a new adventure every year, and our precious little princess daughter was born with a debilitating bone disease. Our strength and resources tested again and again.

But now, it's just me! Hey! Welcome back, Me! I've missed spending time with you. Missed reading books with you, missed listening to music of my own choice with you. I think I'm going to be happy with Me. Now I have a choice: I can share myself with people I love, or I can keep Me all to myself and dance alone for awhile.

I can celebrate the past for what it was, and I can celebrate the present for all its possibilities. I love being Me. In fact, I am really good company. I have fascinating hobbies that I can enjoy for hours. Or, on occasion, I can let a few playmates into my life to enjoy a corner of my wonderful world.

I can walk out into the world a confident, sturdy woman because I have enjoyed my time alone. Because of Me, there is no limit to my enjoyment of life and the enthusiasm I have for living.

Oh, it is true, my energy level isn't what it used to be. But the demands are not what they were either. So when I tire, I sit; no one is waiting for me. I can be quiet and still as long as I need, all hurry-up is gone.

I have survived so much. And perhaps there are more trials to come. But for now, it's Me—good ol' Me, content and living life on my own terms. I have come to accept my solitary life as truly a good way to live.

And that smile you see on my face comes from having made my journey inward—and found myself!

*Then I realized that it is good and proper for a woman to eat and drink, and to find satisfaction in her toilsome labor under the sun during the few days of life God has given her—for this is her lot. Moreover, when God gives any woman wealth and possessions, and enables her to enjoy them, to accept her lot and be happy in her work—this is a gift of God. She seldom reflects on the days of her life, because God keeps her occupied with gladness of heart.*

Paraphrased from Ecclesiastes 5:18–20

*I take enormous pleasure every time I see something that I've done that cannot be wiped out. In some way . . . I guess it's a protest against mortality. But it's been so much fun! It's the curiosity that drives me. It's making a difference in the world that prevents me from ever giving up.* —Deborah Meier

Be it decreed that my life from this point on will be a celebration of my days, not a lament of aging.

*Be it decreed* that the remaining years granted to me will be my most productive years yet and will be my most expressive years—given that I am becoming less impressed by what others think of me.

*Be it decreed* that I will live each day as the wonder it is—having spent previous years searching for who I am and what I am. The search is over; I am now free to live. I am more myself than I ever have been.

*Be it decreed* that I now see aging as a gain rather than a loss because the new age is a span with such meaning and purpose.

*Be it decreed* that I reserve the right to leave the party while it is still fun.

*Be it decreed* that I no longer need to strive to impersonate my younger self. I am quite content to be the elegant age I am.

*Be it decreed* that I will not live in fear or disdain. Both are quite the waste of my valuable time.

*Be it decreed* that my health and my pains remain my private knowledge.

*Be it decreed* that nothing will be forbidden and everything will be permitted, including afternoon naps, staying up late, and eating cheesecake.

*Be it decreed* that I may at any time wear party clothes with all the jewelry I want.

*Be it decreed* that I may use whatever time is necessary, on any given day, to smell the roses.

*Be it decreed* that from this day forward I never will be expected to sit through sensational movies based on creating fake thrills.

*Be it decreed* that I never have to "explain" myself. Doing something "just for the heck of it" is reason enough.

*By irrevocable degree,* be it established that I now enjoy the life of happiness that was impossible as a young woman when I was constantly needed both at home and at work.

*Be it decreed* that I can and will leave the scene of any activity or conversation that no longer holds meaning or purpose.

*Be it decreed* that I will continue to find and accept challenges—to undertake difficult tasks for the sheer joy of it. I will take risks and accomplish what I must to remain a valuable player in the game.

# Afterword

$\mathcal{M}$y friends, I must now go, to return to my daily life. Writing has a way of sheltering you from the world and from normal activities for the duration of the project. I have enjoyed our time together, you and I, talking, thinking, praying, and looking for a deeper understanding of God's love and grace.

As we go, I believe that regardless of what your life circumstances are, your life and my life hold promise and opportunity beyond our wildest dreams. I look forward to every hour and every day of the coming months, and I hope you will too. Life is good.

As we go, I thank you for being my green pastures and my still waters. When I visit with you on paper, I also draw strength from knowing you're there reading. I draw strength for the deep valleys of darkness.

As we go, I enjoy thinking about the time each of us share in Bible study with friends. Our lives are sometimes moving into uncharted waters, and the time we spend encouraging each other is like a team of rowers, learning to all put their oars in the water with a rhythm that propels the boat forward. Assemble yourselves in study.

As we step into our unknown futures, let us go together, and go with God. Your high moments will be my high moments, and your low moments, my lows.

Then, from time to time, we will gather in our green pastures and beside our still waters, until we can again gather the strength to continue.

And always, always, look for special manifestations of His goodness—they will be yours.

My Sunday school class has a ritual each week. When we finish the Bible study each Sunday, we stand in a circle, hold hands, and pray for each other. It creates a strong bond of Christian sisterhood. I want us to do that now. In your mind, think of a vast circle of women standing together. Think of the power of God circulating through each person and moving around the circle. Think of drawing on that grace, that power.

*Most Holy God, Prince of Peace, be born to us again. We bring each woman here into Your presence to experience Your mercy. Grace for us all.*

*Wherever we find pain among us, may we experience strength to endure.*

*Wherever there is loneliness, let there be comfort.*

*Wherever there are feelings of hopelessness, let there be grace and mercy.*

*Wherever there is fear of the future, or fear of the unknown, or fear of failure, give us courage like the courage we feel as we are all here together.*

*Where there is anger and bitterness among us, come, Lord Jesus, with peace and healing.*

*Now, I affirm God as the Source of my life— the Author and the Finisher.*

*I affirm God as Presence—the Keeper, the Sustainer Who works with what He has.*

*I affirm God as Creator—Who always makes life out of my personal chaos.*

*Amen.*

# QUOTATION REFERENCES

Quotations came from many different sources. Some collected through the years; some from new publications. Sources include:

Lisa Bevere. *Be Angry, But Don't Blow It!* Thomas Nelson Publishers, 2000

Jill Brisco. *The Desert Experience*. Thomas Nelson Publishers, 2000

Nancie Carmichael. *The Desert Experience*. Thomas Nelson Publishers, 2000

Karen Dockrey. *When a Hug Won't Fix the Hurt*. New Hope Publishers, 2000

Cheri Fuller. *Trading Your Worry for Wonder*. Broadman & Holman Publishers

Cynthia Heald. *When the Father Holds You Close*. Thomas Nelson Publishers, 1999

Mary Hunt. *The Financially Confident Woman*. Broadman & Holman Publishers, 1996

Margaret Jensen. *Who Will Wind the Clock?* Thomas Nelson Publishers

Anne Morrow Lindberg. *Gift from the Sea*. Pantheon Press, 1991

Beth Moore. *Feathers from My Nest*. Broadman & Holman Publishers, 2001

Victoria Moran. *Creating a Charmed Life*. Harper San Francisco, 1999

Stormie Omartian. *Lord, I Want to Be Whole*. Thomas Nelson Publishers, 2000

Robert Schuller. *Success Is Never Ending: Failure Is Never Final*. Thomas Nelson Publishers

Joni Eareckson Tada. *Ordinary People—Extraordinary Faith*. Thomas Nelson Publishers, 2001

Becky Tirabassi. *Let Prayer Change Your Life*. Thomas Nelson Publishers, 2000

Thelma Wells. *Girl, Have I Got Good News for You*. Thomas Nelson Publishers, 2000

*The Columbia Book of Quotations by Women*. Columbia University Press

Louisa May Alcott

Lillian Carter

Heather Farr

Eva Jessye

Helen Keller

Irena Klepfisz

Diana Nyad

Ellen Henrietta Swallow Richards

Eleanor Roosevelt

Sister Ruth

Anne Howard Shaw

Elizabeth Cady Stanton

# ABOUT THE AUTHOR

*S*UZANNE DALE EZELL is a freelance writer, published in more than thirty periodicals. Her most recent book, *Living Simply in God's Abundance,* chronicles an honest expression of the adventure to find God's purpose through many choices and challenges in a family of five. In everyday life, Suzanne is the director of a senior citizen center and has now added the most esteemed title of all to her bio, that of *grandmother* to two little girls, Abigail and Evelyn.

# OTHER BOOKS BY SUZANNE DALE EZELL

*Living Simply in God's Abundance:*
*Finding Strength and Comfort for the*
*Seasons of a Woman's Life*

The best-selling book *Living Simply in God's Abundance* is a rich tapestry of wisdom from the stories of author Suzanne Dale Ezell and the generations of women who have influenced her. Each day's reading offers insight into the joys and struggles found in the seasons of life and practical advice for managing and cherishing that season. This beautiful book celebrates the unique challenges and opportunities every woman faces and illuminates the essential materials needed to nurture a contented soul and craft a full life.

**ISBN: 0-7852-7063-9**